The Sespe Wild *Environmental Arts and Humanities Series*

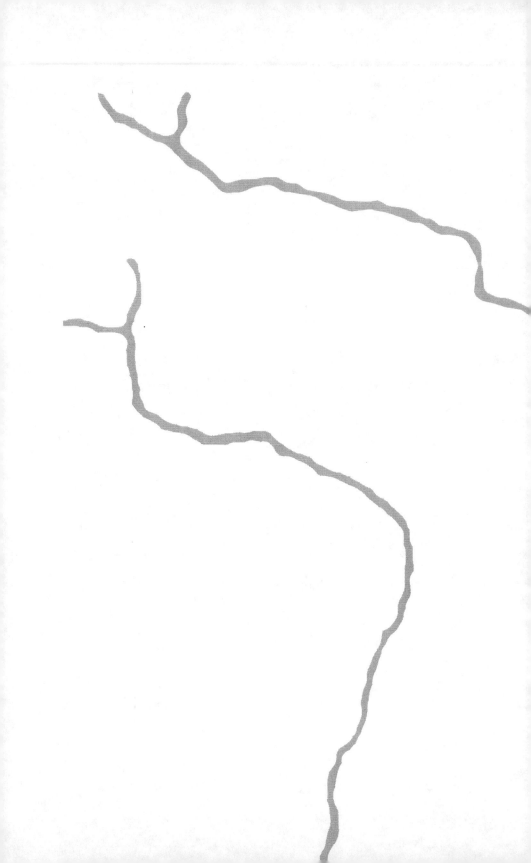

The Sespe Wild

Southern California's Last Free River

BRADLEY JOHN MONSMA

University of Nevada Press ▲▲ Reno & Las Vegas

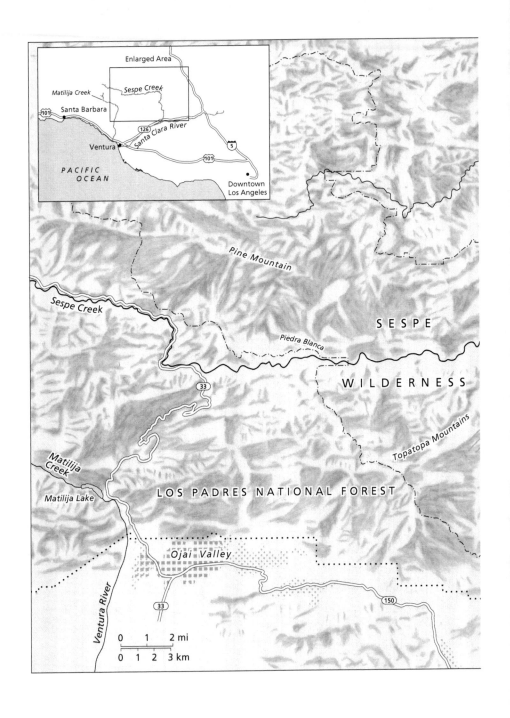

Enlarged Area

Matilija Creek

Sespe Creek

Santa Barbara

101

PACIFIC
OCEAN

Ventura

126

Santa Clara River

5

101

Downtown
Los Angeles

Pine Mountain

Sespe Creek

SESPE

Piedra Blanca

33

WILDERNESS

Matilija
Creek

Topatopa Mountains

Matilija Lake

LOS PADRES NATIONAL FOREST

Ojai Valley

Ventura River

33

150

0   1   2 mi

0   1   2   3 km

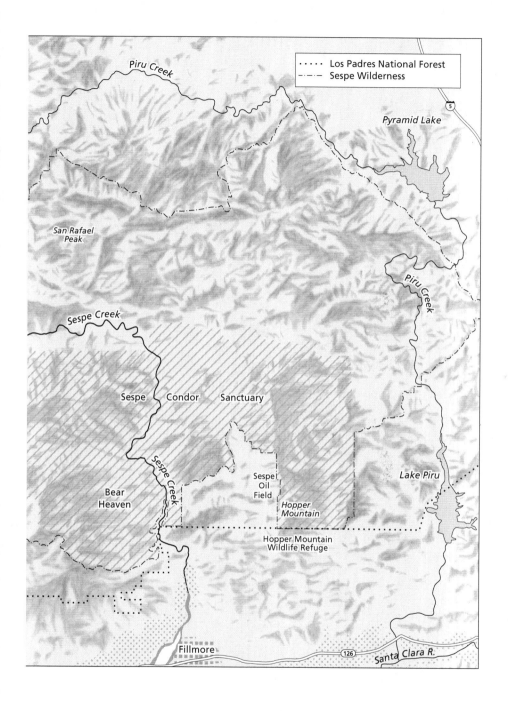

Piru Creek

Los Padres National Forest
Sespe Wilderness

Pyramid Lake

5

San Rafael
Peak

Piru Creek

Sespe Creek

Sespe   Condor   Sanctuary

Sespe
Oil
Field

Lake Piru

Bear
Heaven

Hopper
Mountain

Hopper Mountain
Wildlife Refuge

Fillmore

126

Santa Clara R.

Environmental Arts and Humanities Series

Series Editors: Scott Slovic and Michael Cohen

University of Nevada Press, Reno, Nevada 89557 USA

Manufactured in the United States of America

Design by Carrie House

Library of Congress Cataloging-in-Publication Data

Monsma, Bradley John, 1966–

The Sespe wild : Southern California's last free river /

Bradley John Monsma.

p. cm. — (Environmental arts and humanities series)

Includes bibliographical references.

ISBN 0-87417-536-4 (hardcover : alk. paper) 1. Natural
history—California—Sespe Creek. 2. Natural history—
California—Sespe Wilderness. 3. Sespe Creek (Calif.)—
History. 4. Sespe Wilderness (Calif.)—History. 5. Sespe
Creek (Calif.)—Description and travel. 6. Sespe Wilderness
(Calif.)—Description and travel. 7. Monsma, Bradley John,
1966—Travel—California—Sespe Wilderness. 8. Sespe
Creek (Calif.)—Environmental conditions. 9. Sespe
Wilderness (Calif.)—Environmental conditions. I. Title.
II. Series.

QH105.C2M7 2004

508.794'9—dc22   2004001832

University of Nevada Press Paperback Edition, 2007
ISBN 978-87417-704-6 (paperback : alk. paper)

This book was reproduced as a digital print.

To my mother for her love of water

To my father for his playful spirit

To Brenda for seeing what I would never have thought to look for

Once in a lifetime, if one is lucky, one so merges

with sunlight and air and running water that whole

eons, the eons that mountains and deserts know,

might pass in a single afternoon without discomfort.

The mind has sunk away into its beginnings among

old roots and the obscure tricklings and movings

that stir inanimate things. . . . One can never quite

define this secret; but it has something to do, I am

sure, with common water. Its substance reaches

everywhere; it touches the past and prepares the

future; it moves under the poles and wanders thinly

in the heights of air. It can assume forms of exquisite

perfection in a snowflake, or strip the living to a

single shining bone cast up by the sea.

—LOREN EISELEY, *The Immense Journey*

Contents

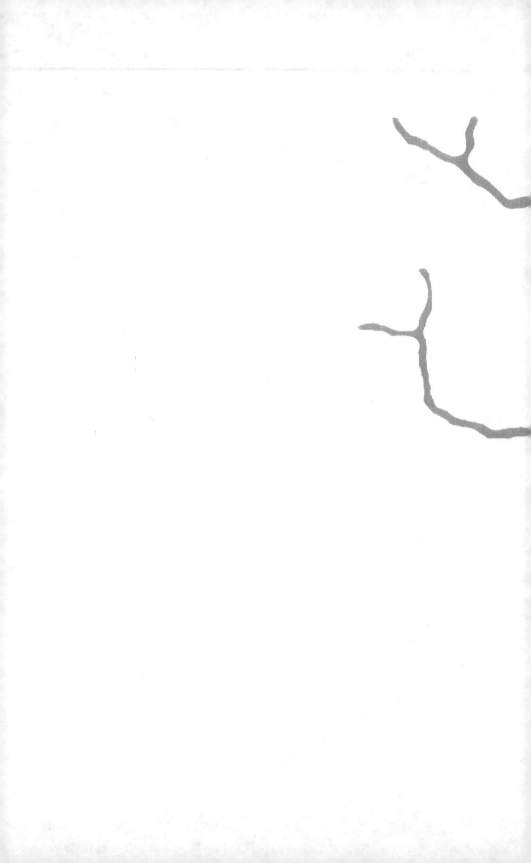

Headwaters

The way of truth is one. But into it, as into a perennial river, streams
flow from all sides. —CLEMENT OF ALEXANDRIA

I've given myself up to a stream for some time now, long enough to know both the necessity and the insufficiency of tracing its currents of story and memory. I've followed its bow bends from one tributary confluence to the next. In clear pools, I've immersed myself and listened to subsurface murmuring. And now I can no more hold the stream in my mind than I can stop its flow through my fingers; yet I'm learning from the way the creek trusts gravity. From springs and snowmelt, the flow follows its path and reshapes its way all at once; outer banks crumble at high water and stones along the streambed tumble into silt. The downstream swiftness seems inexorable but for eddies suspending time and the river for a few moments. An upstream breeze appears to reverse the flow, and refraction displaces the trout shimmering beneath the surface.

How do you begin to know a river? You seek its source. Everyone knows that. You journey to the beginning, preferably enduring travails that sharpen perception and deepen insight. You hope to find the poetry in the outpouring, to sit by a spring and meditate on the path and purposes of the stream from start to finish. In its beginning is its end. You may even risk microbes to take a ceremonial sip from the source and make the stream a part of you. This is how it should begin.

But this isn't how it happened for me. Instead, I chose a day to drive northwest from my home in Los Angeles into the mountains near where maps show Sespe Creek beginning. It was still early when I parked the truck and continued on my bike along a still-frozen fire road that followed a ridge into the chaparral hills. I planned to ride a few miles, then bushwhack down to the source. Things seemed to be going well. The air was crisp, the views long. I needed to breathe deeply and feel muscles working hard. Then the sun began to warm the wet clay road. In a few turns of the wheel, my bike became an earthmover, and I nearly went over the handlebars. Basketball-size glops of clay gathered at the brake pads. When I got off the bike, clay sucked at my shoes, and I stumbled around as if softballs were stuck to my soles. I sighed. Nothing to do but dig in and de-glop. The first three times this happened I retained my patience. The fourth time, I tossed the bike to the side of the road and walked away into a meadow to have a chat with myself. I looked around—for the first time, really. I had just been going along like Coyote—waiting to see what slows me down, waiting to see what sticks.

Below me, the creek's tendrils branched in all directions. v-shaped drainages notched the hills like spread fingers pressed into sand. The map marked one of these fingers as Sespe Creek, but the finger bore no distinction, and the choice looked like the result of a coin flip. Clearly, the Sespe is a watershed before it is a stream. Tiny rivulets from seeps, rain, and snow form dozens of small rills scattered in the slopes. Gradually, disparate waters gather unto themselves to become creeks worthy of naming.

One cannot journey to such a source. One can only piece it together from fragments, gather it from the particulars. Perhaps, by trying to see it from many angles, one might glimpse the wholeness and integrity that lies in dim shadows and swirls in deep eddies. Trying to find the source of such a stream is like trying to find the source of love; the closer you get, the more dispersed and grand it becomes.

One way to see this river I love is through the numbers. Sespe Creek flows for fifty-five miles though some of the wildest, most remote places in California. Yet the mouth of the creek—where the Sespe joins the Santa Clara River—lies less than fifty miles by raven's flight northwest of downtown Los Angeles. The backcountry wanderer will be periodically reminded of the proximity to the city as DC-10s overhead power down and buckle up for the final descent into Burbank. The creek runs through the heart of the 219,700-acre Sespe Wilderness. Compared to the Frank Church River of No Return Wilderness in Idaho—the largest in the lower forty-eight states at 2.4 million acres—the Sespe might seem like a postage stamp. Yet some have called the Sespe the nation's largest roadless area near a metropolis. Los Angeles. Ventura. Thousand Oaks. The Oxnard/Camarillo plain. Santa Barbara. The spreading suburbs north of LA. The Sespe has devotees in all of these places and in Ojai, Santa Paula, and Fillmore, the smaller towns at its borders. Decades ago, the rancher and condor advocate Ian McMillan wrote, "Nor do I know of any other water course anywhere that compares with this wild, twisted, rock-walled canyon. Located, almost in surrealistic fashion, near the northern edge of one of the world's most bizarre metropolitan developments, the crooked Sespe is fantastic beyond anything man has yet constructed" (156). Indeed, the Sespe is the wild heart of Southern California, a next-door wilderness where transformations can happen in a heartbeat or a blink of an eye.

To consider this place, therefore, is to call up issues crucial wherever wilderness and cities meet: recreational impacts on wildlife habitat, the dynamics of accessibility and protection, the physical and psychological need for healthy ecosystems, threats of development and resource extraction. The Sespe—present and past—reminds us that nature and culture have always intermingled.

The Sespe bears a remarkably rich layering of natural and cultural history. Though most of it has been officially designated both wilderness and wild and scenic river, it has never been "untrammeled." The indigenous Chumash, the Spanish padres and soldiers, ranchers, hunters, "anthropologist" grave robbers, serious ethnographers, geologists, miners, oil drillers, dam speculators, pioneering rock climbers and kayakers, hot-springs neopagans, and wilderness activists have all contributed to the stratification of stories. The layers of human history are part of the Sespe's surprising wildness. The narratives of loss we've come to associate almost reflexively with wild places are not adequate to the Sespe. The Sespe also tells a story of ongoing creation and renewal. So close to cities, the Sespe still provides a home to such charismatic species as condors, bighorn sheep, black bears, mountain lions, and steelhead trout, as well as to such less conspicuous creatures as horned lizards, red-legged frogs, and arroyo toads. Roads of thirty years ago are brushy, washed-out trails today. This place exists at the intersection of ecological processes and human ideas for what wilderness should be and do.

The Sespe, last free-flowing stream in Southern California, descends through a geography of hope for both its other-than-human inhabitants and the many people who hold its presence in mind and visit occasionally. The Sespe has escaped the fate of so many rivers throughout the West that have been diverted, impeded, polluted, dammed. It has changed and changed back; its essence remains. For this alone, we should treasure its stories. We should repeat them and be inspired. And as the stories continue to unfold, we should listen and look closely.

The Sespe—creek and wilderness—encourages perception both subtle and expansive, for the backcountry here is an "in-between" place that doesn't meet many expectations. In spots and for moments, the Sespe conjures something akin to the sublimity of the Sierra Nevada and the drama of the Mojave. But it is different. The stream anchors an ecosystem neither alpine nor desert nor coastal; rather, it is all of these—a complex, riverine network of species and processes. Folds of bloodred sandstone lead from riparian intimacies to wind-gnarled juniper on high ridges. The foggy marine layer creeps up the valleys from the ocean only to be burned off, leaving dry chaparral and spring wildflowers. The Sespe keeps the eyes, intellect, and emotions on the move. I suspect more than one person has fallen to his knees before the Topatopa bluffs at sunset and prayed to be transformed into a condor winging up to the day's last warm light. Far below, where deep pools hold the memory and future of steelhead trout, someone might whisper from the shade of an oak, "I'll pick up the pack and start walking . . . in just a minute or two."

But such moments of unmistakable beauty are balanced by claustrophobic trail miles spent between walls of impenetrable chaparral, the vines of wild cucumber entangling the ankles, dust mixing with sweat. Just as your mind focuses too tightly on the relief afforded by the next ridgeline view, you glance down to see a perfect bear print in moist clay or reach toward the softness of blooming woolly blue curls. And then, at a caesura in the steady beat of feet on a long walk, you breathe a mix of scents as complex as a fine meal and nearly as nourishing. Exhaling, you begin to "see" the Sespe as each of the senses connects with the others and your perception widens and flows out into the landscape as the landscape flows in.

As I try to look into the heart of the Sespe, I've found it best not to look too directly. Or, as I follow a line of sight, I try to attend as well to the borders of the visible, the knowable. Think of the value of peripheral vision to athletes and backcountry wanderers. When we say a great hockey center "sees" the ice, we appreciate the extraordinary gift that enables him to participate fully and subtly in an ever changing scene, to anticipate the puck's unlikely carom from the corner. Likewise, the best trail companions are those who see not only the scenic view but also the movements and colors at the corner of the eye. Flashes of light become whole in the imagination. An act of creative participation, the glimpse links what is known to what is suspected.

Seeing—like touch, taste, smell, and hearing—might affirm our fully sensual engagement with our surroundings. I began to learn this early, growing up in northern Michigan with a biology teacher for a father. Sometimes on a Sunday afternoon, Dad would treat my sister and me to perceptual games normally reserved for his high school classes. He would blindfold us, put us in the car, drive in confusing circles, and lead us into the woods somewhere on the outskirts of town. Sightless, our relationship to woods slowed down. The familiar became adventurous, even a little threatening. After a few steps, we dropped to our knees where things were more tangible. Dad didn't stop with just letting us muck around on the forest floor. We had to dig. We had to smell the decomposing leaves. We tried to identify mosses, lichens, and trees by feel. If wintergreen grew nearby, we would chew the minty leaves and red berries. Finally, lying on our backs, we took off our blindfolds to look up at the canopy from an unaccustomed perspective. With the entire experience as context, we would make spyglasses of our hands to discover what photographers know—that precise focus can reveal what before was unnoticed. Yet by attending to all the senses, we began to uncenter our minds from ourselves. Everything came together and began to fall into place.

I learned something similar on one of my first solo hikes in the Sespe, at the start of a long uphill grade. My breathing quickened, and my eyes settled on the trail as usual. At the time, I tended to treat climbs as athletic challenges, and so I picked up the pace as if pain meant gain. Then, a fleeting shadow darkened the ground before me. My feet stopped. My head snapped up. Nothing. Quick glances left and right. Nothing. No sound of an airplane. "*Grronk, brrrruppp, grrrg.*" I spun around to find a raven on the wind, hovering above and behind me, underneath it steady air. As I do with cats in the city, I tried to answer the bird in something like its own language, out of politeness. I hoped it would appreciate the effort even if it couldn't figure out what I was saying. Over the next half mile the raven dogged me, casting its shadow across my own, speaking when I looked up, indulging my garbled ravenese.

"Wake up," called the raven. "Look around. Pay attention. Let your next step be outside yourself. Imagine what this place means to me."

My mind on the wing, I saw the trail stretching out before and behind me. I saw the creek turn south around the corner of the mountain. There was commotion around something dead at the edge of a high meadow. Clouds crowded the peaks. An unseen jet rumbled like thunder. A coyote nosed a rusty oil tank above a creek bed. Frogs slipped through the surface of the stream all at once. The bright bark of manzanita twisted around the gray, dead wood that once was bright. I saw the whole landscape glimmering in a pool and melting down the river's tongue into the next rapid.

I turned and the land turned beneath me. I thought of my home in the city and followed the streets and paths from there to here. With my feet on the ground, I walked toward the Sespe while seeing all around me at once, mind open and empty. Ready for what would come.

Tributaries

CHAPTER 1

In the Eye of a Condor

The Making of a Place

> *My heart in hiding*
> *Stirred for a bird,—the achieve of, the mastery of the thing!*
> —GERARD MANLEY HOPKINS, "The Windhover"

To make the ridge before dark, my friend Mike and I push ourselves up Red Reef Canyon from Sespe Creek, noting along the way the angle of the sun on the Topatopa bluffs in the Sespe Condor Sanctuary. This is the first time I've seen the bluffs up close rather than from the valley floor or from Johnston ridge across the valley miles to the north. On clear days I've often looked up at the Topatopas while kayak surfing at the Silver Strand beach in Oxnard. Now, in my mind's eye I see all the views at once, and the pieces of landscape I've experienced separately become connected. Sespe Creek and the beach made of its sand don't seem so far apart. It all seems to fit in my mind's eye.

On my first hike in the Sespe, my wife, Brenda, and I, along with Mike and another friend, had watched the bluffs at sunset from Willett Hot Springs in a notch on the facing slope. The sight of the glowing rock kept the Sespe on my mind, though other coincidences helped. That night when I got up to pee, I saw Hayakutake comet straight overhead in the only visible patch of sky. Thinking back, I wonder whether I glanced at Cassiopeia, the W-shaped constellation the Chumash see as a condor. Now, years later, after hiking for nine hours, Mike and I crest the ridge as the ruggedness around us reddens. We celebrate the end of the climb with high fives and theme music from the movie *Rocky*, then scramble to snapshoot the fading light. As we catch our breath and savor the scenery, Mike looks at the wild, unapproachable bluffs and remarks with good humor, "If condors can't survive here, they deserve to die. What more can we do for them?"

I don't know what to say, so I chuckle at Mike's candor. It's true that this landscape looks to be the best condors could hope for. We seem to be at the top of the known world, on the verge of taking flight ourselves. We can feel the updraft. If I were alone I would at least stretch out my arms and hop a little to see if I would have the faith to make possible an enskyment. Thirty-six hundred feet below us, Sespe Creek links east with west. Straight ahead, the mountains of the Transverse Ranges stretch the northern horizon. The ridge we stand on seems a fine barrier between the lights flickering on in the Santa Clara and Ojai Valleys at our backs and the darkening wilderness at our feet. The bluffs on our right provide unassailable protection for anything that can perch and disappear into creases and shadows. It seemed a reasonable question. If not here, where? What more could a bird, even one with a nine-foot wingspan, need?

The answer, as it turns out, is more of the same and a few other things as well. So started my attempts to see the Sespe from the perspective of condors. How, I wondered, might my view of this place change if I allowed my imagination to take flight? How would the angles and patterns of the landscape look on the wing? Would my understanding of the overlay of human uses and priorities shift? Would my sense of time in relation to distance change?

It so happened that the Condor Recovery Program had released three condors in the Sespe Condor Sanctuary the month before our hike. Adult Condor 8 and two juvenile males raised at the Los Angeles Zoo had been freed together in hopes that AC-8, an older bird who had been captured wild and was reaching the end of her egg-laying years, would train the younger birds to act like proper condors. Condor experts believed that AC-8 would also remember the topography of her home territory even after nearly fifteen years in captivity. And remember she did, so well that by the time of our hike, she was using historic condor perches and had followed the Tehachapi Mountains on up to the southern Sierra Nevada as she had when she was younger. The two juveniles, B-1 and B-2, couldn't keep up. B-1 flew down the valley near the town of Fillmore along highway 126 where some young people who thought they were helping fed it chicken meat. Since the bird showed signs of habituation to human contact, it was recaptured and returned to the Los Angeles Zoo. B-2 took a sandwich from construction workers, but proved to be independent and a precocious flyer. B-2 did not seek out other human contact and moved on from the release site. With AC-8 and B-2 flying free and far, there were probably no condors in the Sespe Condor Sanctuary when Mike and I were on the ridge looking for them.

Still, even the idea of condors helps me think differently about the sanctuary and about the wilderness generally. Consider two perspectives on distance. Mike and I began our hike by walking through the middle of the sanctuary at its narrowest point, about three miles by flight. By the end of our three-day, thirty-mile walk and the car shuttle, we had circumnavigated the western two-thirds of the sanctuary. In contrast, condors can glide at fifty-five miles per hour and range three hundred miles in a day on the lookout for dead deer, cattle, ground squirrels, or defrosting calves left by Fish and Wildlife. The same space that seemed nearly endless to Mike and me as we measured it foot by plodding foot might appear relatively small in the eyes of a condor on high. Our 3,600-foot climb could be done on the wing in a blink and a breath of wind. The sanctuary, about thirteen miles at its widest boundaries, might be an occasional home, but only the beginning of the whole neighborhood needed for a full condor life.

Attempting to see the lay of the land through the eye of the condor quickly turns a wide-angle wilderness view into a lesson in the limitations that we impose on other species. I've tried to see the Sespe as a condor might by sitting on Topatopa ridge and glancing between the terrain and a map. Both views give me altitude. Neither helps me know what a condor would notice or focus on. The map especially, with its layers of boundary lines, tells me more about the way people see this place, indeed how people have created this place. Only on the map can I see the distinct lines separating the Sespe Condor Sanctuary from the Sespe Wilderness and the official wilderness from the Los Padres National Forest. Cross-hatchings mark scattered private inholdings. The boundary lines represent the results of political and philosophical struggles. They signify who owns portions of the landscape and who manages its resources. They tell me who can use the land and in what manner. On the map the landscape appears under control and orderly. Sometimes I wonder whether maps don't help us fool ourselves into thinking we know enough to control the land completely.

Looking at the terrain itself, I see undulating waves of brush broken by stands of trees and outcroppings of sandstone. It all seems of a piece even as I turn to the south to see the towns of the Santa Clara and Ojai Valleys. In simplest terms, the Sespe seems smaller and less isolated when I cruise with condors in my daydreams. On the wing, I can't maintain the illusion of the Sespe as a world apart as I can when I'm trudging for miles along the creek. The condor's eye casts a realistic glance down on my wilderness. My grounded, down-to-earth perspective turns out to be more a figment of my imagination than flight dreams.

The shadows of California condors (*Gymnogyps californianus*) have moved over the Sespe for thousands of years. Only for a short period between 1987, when the last wild condor was captured, and 1992, when birds hatched and raised in captivity began to be released into the wild, were condors and the land separated. During the last century, as humans have drawn boundary lines on the landscape, condors have persisted in flying right over and through them. The condors ignore our arrangements even though, from our perspective, some of the boundaries owe their existence to the birds.

I first heard the name Carl Koford in the offices of the U.S. Fish and Wildlife Service in Ventura from an official with the Condor Recovery Program. "You need to know that name," he told me. "The Sespe wilderness exists because of Carl Koford." True enough, I discovered as I read about Koford's early condor research. But the more I read, the more I found it interesting that someone from the Condor Recovery Program had pointed me toward Koford, for he had vehemently opposed the captive breeding program and intensive management now overseen by the U.S. Fish and Wildlife Service. Perhaps the program can so comfortably point to its opponents of the past because it has been, by many measures, a success. The total population of California condors in the world has risen from its lowest level of 22 in 1983 to 208 in July of 2002. Since 1992, the program has been reintroducing condors in California and Arizona, where there are between seventy and eighty birds in the wild. The number of birds is steadily rising, though occasionally they die of various natural and unnatural causes. The photogenic releases draw crowds of journalists and typically receive extensive coverage in newspapers throughout California and on the local and national TV news. For millions, the success of the Condor Recovery Program is confirmed by the news clips of AC-8 soaring gracefully from the release cage to a cliff-side perch while her pupils botch the attempt to follow and opt instead for an easier perch in the top of a tree. Follow-up reports detail the power line and human avoidance therapy all birds undergo before release. Reporters follow field biologists who drag frozen calves into the backcountry to ensure food sources free from lead shot. The biologists, monitoring the birds with radio telemetry units, testify to their love for them and explain how each bird has a unique "personality" and role in the social hierarchy of condors. This season, the birds are watched carefully for courtship behavior in hope of the first wild mating and nesting since the reintroductions began.

Neither have condors gone extinct from the minds of Southern Californians. Recently, the San Diego Wild Animal Park has been advertising its newest show, "Condor Ridge," in which it displays captive birds to the public and explains the institution's role in the condor's recovery to date. A Los Angeles theater company has named itself after the bird, as has the ice hockey team in Bakersfield. Imagine a goalie with a nine-foot wingspan.

For the presence of condors in our skies and imaginations, we owe much to Carl Koford's attempts to estimate the extant population and outline threats to condor survival in the Sespe region beginning in 1939. Koford's effort was single-handed and heroic. Before grant money paid for an old Model T Ford, he regularly hiked a steep twelve miles through difficult terrain down to the town of Fillmore for supplies. Much of the research consisted of sitting in blinds observing nests in all kinds of weather, from wasting heat to snowstorms. In an interview late in his life he displayed the sort of even temperament that absorbed backcountry hardship:

> It was not really bad country because there was water in the
> potholes, so you didn't have to carry water. Normally, you
> know, you drink a gallon a day in hot country. It was the
> brush—learning how to get through the scrub oak and
> stuff—that was difficult. We didn't have mountain boots
> or anything like that in those days, but I got some logging
> boots with hobnails and they worked pretty well on the rocks.
> I wore out two or three pairs of those. (Phillips and Nash 67)

I once heard subsequent condor researcher John Borneman tell the story of how in the 1960s he found a remote observation point he called "Koford's Cave." He picked up an old milk bottle from the floor of the cave and remarked with some reverence, "Koford drank from this." When he told this to Koford years later, Koford smiled. "I used to pee in that bottle."

One result of Koford's hard work was that he developed a characterization of condor behavior that supported the idea of a special sanctuary. Even though he had often visited active nests and handled chicks, he began to portray condors as extremely shy and susceptible to disturbance. In contrast, some earlier condor researchers had described the bird as remarkably tolerant of human intrusion, often allowing photography close to nests without the use of blinds. Koford's views, however, became the conventional wisdom on condors and served as the basis of a logical chain of reasoning about the best way to forestall extinction. Since condor numbers were declining and human intrusion might be to blame, it stood to reason that the best way to save condors was to preserve habitat and thereby keep people away from the birds. According to Noel and Helen Snyder, authors of a recent and comprehensive book on the California condor, Koford's notes and correspondence indicate that the idea of a sanctuary was there from the beginning of his research (64). And in 1947, the Sespe Condor Sanctuary was established.

Later, in the 1980s, land preservationists working to establish what was then called the Sespe-Frazier Wilderness quickly recognized the possibilities of the converse: the best way to save habitat was to focus on condors. A charismatic, endangered bird might sway public opinion and become a symbol of the need to protect wildlands. Gradually, the condor became an emblem in the fight to preserve wilderness "untrammeled by man." Ultimately, the bird and the land became one. The symbolism was crucial, since the fight for wilderness designation was occurring simultaneously with the controversy about whether to remove birds from the wild to begin a captive-breeding program. Wilderness activists feared that once condors were absent from the proposed wilderness areas, the general public would see no reason to protect their habitat. The famed wilderness activist David Brower, whose organization Friends of the Earth opposed capturing wild condors, described the connection with his typically pithy phrasing: "A condor is five per cent feathers, flesh, blood, and bone. All the rest is *place*" (Phillips and Nash 275).

If activists' use of the condor as symbol seems self-serving, it is important to remember that the area of Koford's early research in the Sespe was repeatedly threatened over the course of a century. The Sespe region near the town of Fillmore had been the site of oil exploration and extraction since the late 1880s, and even after the sanctuary was established, mineral leasing was not withdrawn until the 1970s (Snyder and Snyder 64). There was also periodic talk of damming Sespe Creek to provide water for agriculture and development in the Santa Clara Valley. For various reasons, dam projects begun in 1915, 1925, 1932, and 1957 failed. In 1967, a $90 million bond issue proposed by the United Water Conservation District for the purpose of damming the stream failed by thirty-nine votes. Wilderness designation and wild and scenic river status for Sespe Creek did not happen until 1992. More on this story later.

Threats to both the condor and its habitat led to the intense debates in the 1980s around the question of whether to capture the remaining wild birds for a captive-breeding program. To one side, the very existence of the species was at stake. Failure to act would be irresponsible, given that humans had already had such devastating impacts. To the other, taking condors from the wild would be to act with hubris and arrogance about our interventions in ecosystems. Captive breeding of a wilderness icon would be a step toward a time when all wildness would be regulated, monitored, and controlled.

In an essay in the 1981 book-length argument against captive breeding, *The Condor Question: Captive or Forever Free?* Koford outlines the reasons why capturing condors would irreparably harm their chances for survival: physiological and psychological stress, disturbance of nests, and danger to dependent young when adults are taken. He warns that one should not generalize from the captive breeding of other species to that of condors. He calls for land acquisitions, better law enforcement to prevent shooting, research into food contamination (researchers had yet to grasp the importance of lead poisoning), and preservation of existing habitat. Koford's conclusion, though, indicates the shift in conservation from a single-species approach to an emphasis on biodiversity: "Apart from the shaky biological basis for captive breeding of condors, the wild condor must be seen as an integral part of a total ecosystem. Protection of the condor and its ecosystem is possible, but only if given the proper emphasis rather than focusing on the removal of condors from the wild" (Phillips and Nash 25).

Ironies abound. Those who argued most forcefully against removal and captive breeding suggested that the scientific research on condors was incomplete and that in our ignorance we had best preserve land and let condors do their thing as they always had. Hindsight suggests that their position was also based on incomplete knowledge of condor mortality, especially of the role of lead poisoning and power line collisions. It would seem now that even had the greatest possible area been given the highest degree of protection, condors may still have become extinct without the captive breeding. It is entirely possible that had opponents of the condor program prevailed, the condor may have made the dignified exit some suggested was the best course in bad times. On the other hand, it is in part due to the efforts of these activists and the condor's charisma that we now have protected wilderness areas so near massive cities in a growing state. We also have largely intact ecosystems home to many creatures other than condors. Places preserved with condors in mind provide hope for other endangered species—the southern steelhead, the red-legged frog and arroyo toad, the bighorn sheep—as well as less charismatic, less threatened creatures. In some ways, the condor debuted the role later played by the spotted owl in the Pacific Northwest.

I'm grateful that both the wilderness advocates and the Condor Recovery Program have been at least initially successful. Without them I doubt I would ever have had the chance to stand along the banks of the last free-flowing stream in Southern California and hope realistically to see condors in free flight. The dilemmas remain palpable, however. I believe that humans have the responsibility, given our impact on the world, to do our best to keep things running smoothly, sometimes through hands-on intervention that gets messy as we work within the limitations of our knowledge. Yet I can't deny my sympathy for the point of view that cautions against overmanagement. A world in which every animal has a number, location, and medical file seems soulless to me, and not outside the realm of possibility given our present trajectory.

While habitat preservation may not have been the only key to saving condors from extinction, it is still true that the birds need space for all their activities and life phases. And if there is one thing precious in Southern California, after water, it is space. In all directions around Los Angeles, battles rage over how "open" spaces ought to be used and whose needs ought to take priority. These battles become dramatically important to seeing the Sespe from the point of view of condors. Historically, condors have used the Sespe region primarily for courtship, breeding, and nesting, yet their best foraging habitat lies outside the Sespe.

Even with the artificial feeding carried out by the recovery program, condors occasionally find a dead cow or deer to the south on Newhall Ranch. The condors land and tear into the carrion unaware that the soil under their feet is highly contested. The earthmoving has begun for what might become a 22,000-home "community," complete with schools and shopping centers and many fewer dead cattle. To the north, Tejon Ranch is also crucial condor foraging habitat. As the largest private continuous land area in Southern California, its 270,000 acres outsize the 220,500 acres of the Sespe Wilderness and Condor Sanctuary combined. A diagram of these vast holdings looks like an inverted funnel through which condors flying from the south might flow naturally into the southern Sierra Nevada. This is due to the natural terrain. For centuries, condors have followed the classic u-shape of terrain from the Coast Range to the east-west running Transverse Ranges and toward the Sierra to the north. Many records dating back to the Spanish colonial era report condors feeding on the high open fields now part of the ranch. It may be that the introduction of livestock to the region affected condors in much the same way it did grizzly bears, providing a consistent source of food and spiking populations. As the numbers of native ungulates declined, cattle and horses more than filled in the gap. To point this out is to acknowledge that condor habitat in Southern California has been "unnatural" for centuries even if you discount the effects that indigenous peoples may have had on bird populations. This fact does not diminish the importance of ranch land for the condors that are left. If the Condor Recovery Program is ever to achieve its stated goal of a wild, self-sustaining population of condors, foraging habitat must be protected.

But once again, what seems obvious in the eye of a condor on the wing gets complicated on the ground, where reality and illusion intertwine. Take Tejon Ranch, for example. Where the condors see rolling oak grasslands and a wild path leading to the Southern Sierra, humans see a layering of stories shaping how we might use the land. This is not unusual, for all landscape, even the deepest wilderness, is inscribed with memory if you go back far enough and look close enough. But the stories I see written on Tejon Ranch don't grow from the land; they don't shape people to the reality of the place. Rather, these stories seek to shape the land and history to our desires. The "ranch" is a recent example of the paradoxes Californians have cultivated since at least as far back as the middle of the nineteenth century. With the missions, the gold rush, the railroads, and countless local events, California has promoted itself by creating mythic histories to barter for residents, tourists, and investors. Simulations, which so often seem initially more attractive than what they stand in for, make a constructed past available for consumption. They put the past up for sale. This is still going on.

The Tejon Ranch logos seamlessly tie ranching nostalgia—"since 1843" the "Gateway to Southern California"—to a clear appeal to its future as "a diversified real estate development and agribusiness company." The mythic history and financial reality come together most clearly with regard to livestock operations. Though livestock no longer seems the focus or priority of the corporation, it is important to setting the scenery for its other, more ambitious and financially rewarding developments. The Web site shows images of cowboys on horseback herding cattle in the sunset while the text explains that forty thousand head of beef are grazed on ranch land and then shipped to a feedlot in Texas. This feedlot is "part of an overall forward integration strategy designed to create a source-verifiable brand of beef known for quality, safety, and consistency." These cowboys learned to write in MBA programs.

As Tejon Ranch's livestock operation becomes ever more decorative, a simulation of its past meant to evoke regional flavor, the condors will have fewer options for real flavor in their diets. Recently, however, the ranch has partnered with a public lands organization to determine the worth of one hundred thousand acres and to find a buyer who will preserve it as wilderness. It is too early to tell how this will work, but it appears that the preservation may be meant to mitigate the corporation's plans for a small city and a resort.

Daily, suburban Los Angeles marches north along Interstate 5. Lookalike subdivisions spring up with breathtaking rapidity to bisect the condor's historical foraging range. Standing alongside the Topatopa bluffs inside the condor sanctuary, it's easy for a person to see these developments as remote. But if that person ascends to the imagined view of the condor, the vastness of the terrain shrinks and the lines on the map disappear. The sanctuary, the wilderness, and the national forest blend together in the eyes of their most recognizable indicator species. What's more, these areas of varying degrees of protection meld with unprotected areas that few people other than condor researchers or those with long memories would associate with the birds at all.

These images and dilemmas clutter my mind as I tag along with U.S. Fish and Wildlife biologist Mike Barth of the Condor Recovery Program. We're tracking two birds he knows are in the Hopper Mountain National Wildlife Refuge, and I'm eager to see my first condor in the wild. When I meet him, Mike reminds me of the ads for the Pony Express: "Wanted: Young, Strong, Wiry Fellows." He speaks with the casualness I associate with Southern California beach culture, and it turns out he surfs. Not that he uses surfer slang too often. It's more a conversational patience, an understatement inflected with a touch of irony. He has a way of making factual statements in a tone that merely hints at his own interpretation: "Two weeks ago AC-8 came down from the Southern Sierra and flew around with these guys for a couple days before heading back up." Then he'll pause a beat to gauge my response—to see if I am suitably impressed. Just as I murmur a "hmmm" or a soft "wow," he'll look sidelong at me, nodding a little and raising his eyebrows in admiration for the bird. Even though Mike's the expert, his timing allows us to share the experience of the birds.

After meeting in a supermarket parking lot in Fillmore, we drive up the long switchbacks carved from the sides of the mountain. We pass numerous oil wells and eventually drive by Carl Koford's cabin perched on a ridge, a tin roof barely held up by weathered boards. Someone has placed a realtor's OPEN HOUSE sign out front. From here I look back down to the sandy wash of the Santa Clara River and think it would be a hard day's work to walk up with a pack. We stop by a grassy slope with a good view of Hopper Canyon, and I sit down on a mound of dirt so I can use my knees to stabilize my binoculars. Mike pulls out the telemetry gear and swings the antenna around to get a fix on the birds. "They're in the air," he says. We both swing binoculars in the direction suggested by the telemetry beeping.

Now I am in familiar territory. I've become an expert at looking for condors without seeing them. A regular feature of my backcountry Sespe walking is the fleeting, soon-to-be-dashed hope conjured by a shape in motion in the corner of my eye. "It's a bird, it's a plane, it's . . ." Today, as I scan the sky, knowing this time that condors are somewhere in it, I see specks of passenger jets descending toward Burbank. This is the same flight path I see through the windows of classrooms where I teach nature writing. When I ask Mike whether experienced condor trackers ever mistake airplanes for birds, he tells me of a "Condor Eye Chart" someone put up in the Fish and Wildlife office. A profile of a condor takes the place of the big "E," and as the chart descends into rows of smaller figures, condors mix with hawks, eagles, airplanes, butterflies, and bumblebees.

After a few false alarms, I spot something. A speck rising on a thermal. I count off fourteen seconds between the bow bends of its turns. Red-tailed hawks will make tighter turns. This bird seems to have the steadiness in the air Mike says is unique to condors. "That's a condor," Mike confirms. "And there's the other below." The two are a potential breeding pair, with the female having spent much of the past year in the area and the male more recently arrived. We watch them break out of the thermal and head south at an astounding pace. I glance down to write a few sentences in my notebook and lose track of them. They reappear in a different section of sky on the other side of a mountain ridge, heading north now, still specks. One catches another thermal and looks exceptionally striking against a cloudbank stacked up over the mountains. The pair splits for a while, then reunites. Mike hopes their behavior might be the start of courtship. "I'd like to think R-12 is giving R-7 the grand tour," he remarks. "I know she knows all sorts of great spots out here. Caves to get out of the weather, good roosts, water holes, nest sites."

I try to concentrate on the condors, but we're sitting in the middle of what appears to be a raptor heaven, and there's lots going on at close range. Mike identifies the flybys at a glance. A pair of northern harriers works the ridge above and behind us. A golden eagle glides in from the right and tucks its wings into a stoop toward a perch in a burned walnut tree below. Ravens case the joint. A keening American kestrel harasses a red-tail trying to rest in a snag. "He's a wannabe peregrine," jokes Mike.

Then, casually, Mike says, "I think they're going to come check us out." I look back at the condors but can't see much to indicate a change in attitude, altitude, or direction. "You might want to get your camera." Then I see that the birds are pointed right at us, moving at freeway speed from a couple of miles away. I dash a few yards to the truck and back just in time to see the pair duck behind a wrinkle in the landscape. Out of view for a few moments, they "stealth" us, appearing suddenly overhead where they slow to gaze at us, their brilliant white underwings flashing. I snap a few shots, then simply stand awestruck, receiving the gift of their presence and offering my heart in return. After a moment they turn, matching the falling angle of the landscape before catching an updraft, specks in the sky again heading south. Mike and I are silent for a minute or two until, looking sidelong at me, he raises his eyebrows and nods a little. I laugh and hoot and hop and bless him for his telepathic condor-calling powers. "I always do my best," he says.

By late afternoon, based on telemetry signals, the pair appears to have landed somewhere in Hopper Canyon. We move to a small grass plateau for a better view of the canyon and look for them with binoculars and a spotting scope. The light softens as the wind suggests evening chill, and Mike shows the patience of an experienced fieldworker. Spotting the roosting birds seems hopeless to me, but Mike keeps looking. "This canyon screams 'condors.'" He focuses on two lumps on a rock outcropping, and we take turns at the scope and debate the shape, size, and possibility. A half hour later, the lumps haven't moved a centimeter. Hearing a high-pitched wind whistle, we both look up as a red-tail in full stoop zips a few feet above our heads and on down the ridge at maybe seventy miles per hour. "Intense. He was showing off." I can't help but make the comparison to a jet fighter. Top gun. I think of how in my life I've seen more military jets in California wilderness than diving red-tails.

I turn to take in the oaks silhouetted against the skyline in the west. A foggy marine layer moving inland now covers the Channel Islands, which earlier had seemed impossibly close to the mainland. The day's last shadow moves up the opposite side of Hopper Canyon, and we pack up the telemetry equipment and scope.

On the way to the ranch house where we'll spend the night, Mike opens a gate as a Cooper's hawk swoops unseen at his back. We catch a glimpse of a black-shouldered kite. We pass the upper pasture where Ari Hopper, namesake of the canyon and the refuge, baited grizzlies in the last decades of the nineteenth century. Back at the ranch, I break out a couple of my home-brewed Belgian ales, and over supper Mike and I talk of surfboard preferences, wave characteristics, and the reliability of surf reports.

In considering Mike's obvious feel for the condors, it occurs to me that the skills of bird-watching and wave-waiting might be related to each other. Both combine intuition and practiced skill. In both, experience seems to make coincidence more likely. I've often sat in the swells and watched the surfers most familiar with the break paddle toward the horizon even when I see no visual cues that a set might be coming in. I've learned to follow them. They've been waiting there, sometimes for decades, in different combinations of tide, wind, swell direction, and season. The best surfers develop observational powers they could never explain. Variables register as intuition and translate into a physical response in seconds. It's not by chance that some surfers get more and better waves than others. On days when few waves break, surfers wait anyway, consoling themselves with the angle of light, the breeze, the glide and plunge of pelicans, and the feeding of dolphins, imbuing themselves more thoroughly with the rhythms of the ocean.

So it is with those who watch birds. They watch the birds and everything else to see the completeness of the scene. Yet they don't just watch. They open their senses to a richness that includes birds.

Maybe a similar dynamic between experience and intuition was behind Mike's telepathic condor call. Waves or birds, such seeking might be understood as a form of creativity in which the seeker involves his whole being in the search even while relinquishing control. The seeker, despite bringing knowledge and experience to bear (not to mention a telemetry unit), knows that the appearance of the wave or bird is a gift that cannot be earned.

As so often happens, when we look long and hard for something, it appears to us in the partly cloudy sky of our dreams. When I tell Mike I had slept badly the night before and awakened with vague memories of condor dreams, he tells me of his own dream:

> I've had flight dreams ever since I was a little kid. Usually I have to concentrate real hard to stay in the air. In one dream some kids on a playground throw their ball outside the fence. I go to get it for them, but a wizardlike man with a flowing beard gets there first. He tosses the ball to me, then turns me into a bird. So soon I'm up soaring around with the condors over the potreros up north where we release them. I was concentrating and focusing. I was so happy to be up there with them. Then one of our trucks comes around the hill, and I think, Oh no, they'll see me! And I'm not supposed to be flying around with the birds. As soon as I think this I lose focus and start to drop. I eat shit in the potrero and come up completely covered with grass. Foxtails are stuck all over my clothes. . . . Just about everyone I know who works with condors dreams about them eventually.

As Mike talks, I remember a story by Gerald Haslam called "Condor Dreams" that flips things around. Instead of humans dreaming of birds, an old man in the story understands reality itself as the dream of a great condor. As long as there are condors, the world goes on.

The next day, dream worlds become more distant as I watch the condors feed on a couple of stillborn calves donated by a big dairy farm in the Central Valley. From a half mile away through the spotting scope, I can see tufts of white calf fur flying as the condors try to dig their way in. My attempt to see from the birds' perspective stalls as I take a bite of my lunch and feel a touch of the long-standing revulsion humans often have toward carrion eaters, especially vultures. After five years with condors, Mike thinks it's cool. "First, they'll eat the tongue," he explains, "then one will usually go to the anus and start pulling things out from there. In a big group, one might grab an organ and run with it. They'll pull out the spine and generally turn the skin inside out." Yum.

With a calf apiece, this pair takes their time, knowing they will get their fill. But the theatrics start when a pair of golden eagles take a reconnaissance flight overhead, then dive-bomb the carcass. The condors both duck. The female eagle is nearly as big as the condors and more aggressive. Eagles may occasionally kill condors, but Mike tells me that R-12, the female condor, has recently gotten the best of the female eagle. After a while, R-7 takes off, its orange-pink crop—an onboard food storage compartment—parting the feathers on its breast. This leaves R-12 to deal with the two eagles that now land and approach the carrion. R-12 spreads her wings and rushes the nearest eagle, leading with her feet and hacking with her beak. Perhaps her size compensates for her lack of sharp, grasping talons, for after a brief, feathery tussle, the eagles back off. Mike cheers softly. He tells me that feeding sites are often action-packed. Coyotes will try to sneak a meal. Ravens will work their trickery, pulling on a condor's tail feathers or rising in unison to spook the condors into taking off. The ravens then fall to eating while the condors have to glide in a big circle to get back to the carcass. Today, R-12 feeds some more, then leaves the carcasses to the eagles. She soon heads up Hopper Canyon to join R-7 and to roost out of our view for the night.

The next morning, Mike and I go to the top of Hopper Mountain to try to find the roosting condors before they take flight. But instead of looking for the condors, I'm thinking again of how this place looks to them. Mike's combinations to locked gates have brought me to where I can look down on the eastern portion of the Sespe Wilderness. "Pretty bitchin' view," he says. I look west down across the oil fields, where deer graze beside wells, to the inaccessible creeks of Bear Heaven slanting down toward the Sespe. My eyes follow the uplift and folds of the Topatopa Mountains and the entire run of the West Fork of Sespe Creek. Miles to the northwest I see the potreros adjacent Johnston Ridge where I hiked to look for bighorn sheep the week before. Mike points out the path of ridges condors follow to the west and then north to the Ventana Wilderness surrounding Big Sur. Turning to the north, I squint to shield the reflection of the sun off the bright sandstone of Whiteacre Peak and the Arundell Cliffs, where the Condor Recovery Program maintains a release site. A line in the chaparral marks where a 1997 fire stopped just before taking out the release structures. Across the Piru Creek drainage I can generally place Interstate 5, and I imagine I'm AC-8 crossing over the freeway, looking for downed cattle on the Tejon Ranch and slipping over the Tehachapi Mountains to see the southern Sierra Nevada beckoning. What I can't imagine is that before too long, AC-8 will be dead, shot down by a pig hunter on Tejon Ranch. Layer of a dozen eggs, her genetic legacy will continue, but the young birds won't have the living example of a condor that knows how to be wild. The hunter will eventually be found, brought to trial, and sentenced to six months probation and a twenty-thousand-dollar fine.

From atop Hopper Mountain I get a visual sense of the whole u-shape of historic condor range. To the southeast, however, hangs the hazy reminder of the metropolis. Mike says that he can see the skyscrapers of downtown Los Angeles on clear days and that if he can see them, so can condors. I ask whether the birds, being curious creatures, have ever shown inclination to explore urban areas easily within a day's round-trip flight. For whatever reason, they don't very often, though one condor recently died of unknown causes in the Santa Susanna Mountains about halfway between here and there. Another time hang gliders over the San Fernando Valley reported condors flying ten feet off their wings and mimicking their turns. The image is fitting. As species, we may find that we fly best together. Nearly forty years ago, rancher Ian McMillan eyed the growth of Los Angeles and, in a book called *Man and the California Condor,* wrote "Ultimately the Sespe Sanctuary, if it remains an inviolate area set aside for condors, will serve equally as a most practicable measure of restraint and control, protecting man's habitat from ecological bankruptcy. Ultimately, condor preservation helps to assure human survival" (158).

I try to consider why I find it jarring to think of a condor looking from downtown LA toward the heart of the Sespe with a turn of its pinkish, featherless head. I compare the view of the condor to my typical experience of leaving the city, turning onto ever smaller, bumpier roads, then hiking behind mountain ridges through brush and canyons. For me, the topography can reinforce the imaginative distance I sometimes seek when I head into the bush. Through physical effort and time, I manage to sever ties between the two places that most influence my life. Whether this disconnection renews or deludes may be a matter of frequency and degree. My grounded perception allows for an illusion condors may not so easily afford. Yet my attempt to see through condor eyes might be the act of discipline that conditions my appreciation of the Sespe.

CHAPTER 2

Escape Habitat

The Return of the Bighorns

The vigorous, the healthy, and the happy survive and multiply.

—CHARLES DARWIN

Condors aren't the only miraculous life along the Sespe, so I take an early morning path from my back door to the world of the Sespe's desert bighorn sheep. I'm never quite sure whether my route traces my own escape and confirms the distance between city and wilderness or whether it demonstrates their proximity and interdependence. The question plays in the back of my mind as I get ready to leave. Mostly, I just don't want to forget anything crucial, like the boots stashed in the corner of the garage still dirty from the last trip. The sheep cross my sleepy mind. It seems unlikely that there are still places wild enough for them to eat, grow, and reproduce on their own, without radio collars and management plans. The LA sky glows streetlight orange, and it seems surreal and dreamlike to think I may see sheep so nearby in just a few hours.

Nevertheless, in the mid-November cold and dark, I toss my pack, poles—and boots—into the back of the truck. As the engine warms for a few moments, I remember the cup of coffee I set on the roof and crank the window open to retrieve it. The neighborhood is mostly asleep as I start out, but the activity quickens and converges as I near the freeway on-ramp. Even at 5:30 A.M. the commuters and haulers are up to speed and intense, presenting a problem for a fifteen-year-old four-cylinder truck. I lean forward to urge it into fifth gear in the slow lane as the double-bottomed tractor trailer behind me hits the brakes at seventy miles per hour. Fifteen minutes later I sip the last of my coffee as I glide down into Santa Clarita, where most of the traffic is headed the other way into the city. The tangled erector sets of Magic Mountain amusement park sit silent this early, and I keep driving up the Grapevine and into the mountains. I downshift. My pace up the mountain is only a little faster than that of the bulldozers grading plots for new houses lining the interstate. I remember an old folksong about little boxes made of ticky-tacky looking all the same. Those houses were made of different colors, but in this subdivision, only beige will be acceptable. Brighter hues will be outlawed by the neighborhood association to protect sacred property values.

I touch the back of my hand to the window glass as I pass the 4,000-foot sign. Ice-cold. Below freezing. I exit at Frazier Park and head inland to approach the Sespe from the north. I drive through dry stands of pine and wide meadows. In the rising sun, the sagebrush sparkles with frost as though strewn with diamonds. Around 7:30, after fourteen miles of dirt road and stream crossings, I arrive at the trailhead and reluctantly kill the engine, my last source of artificial heat. I put my cap on and tie my boots extra tight to keep my toes from jamming on the seven-mile, 2,500-foot descent. Pack on, I begin the walk. Cold quail wait for the nearest footfall to flush from sagebrush and dried lupine.

I cross a meadow and begin the descent. Snow lines the trail in the shadows, mixing with the plumed seeds of mountain mahogany to form an inch of fluff. I pause in a sunny spot for the first expansive view of the Sespe backcountry. Far below stony bluffs and peaks, Sespe Creek courses through chaparral folds broken by protrusions of sandstone. The landmarks remind me of other walks and of other reasons for walking. A western flycatcher flits to a bush an arm's length away and tilts its head at me for a few moments.

The chaparral thins out as I descend south into the sun. Dry stalks of yucca hold their seed-bells high for the wind. I swing a hiking pole to thwack one, and hundreds of seeds rattle and scatter in all directions, including down my shirt and into my hair. Weeks later the seeds will turn up in odd places in my house. Deer trails cross the loose, pea-grain gravel resting at the angle of repose. I walk the knife-edge ridgeline. Bright cottonwoods line the canyon stream to my right, trailing toward its confluence with Hot Springs Creek on my left before together they join Sespe Creek.

The trail drops just off the ridgeline to hide me from view of the canyon where the sheep might be. I pop my head over the top every so often to glass the opposite cliffs and slopes, but so far I've seen nothing. Finally, I give up on the binoculars, opting for a wide-angle view. And there, just above the hot springs, I see a flash at the edge of my vision. A cute white butt pointing right at me. The next moments are a fine imitation of a hunter's buck fever. My heart rate rises. My hands tremble slightly. I try to fumble for binoculars without moving. I sit down for a steadier hand. Lost her. After rescanning the rock for five minutes, I find her calmly munching mountain mahogany.

Just six hours have passed since I kissed sleeping Brenda, locked my back door, and stood for moment listening to the city already humming through the predawn chill.

Even people familiar with the Sespe backcountry are surprised to learn of the mountain sheep on the slopes above the creek. Truly, their presence is something of a miracle, a testament to the rejuvenative grace of wild places. Once lost, now found, sheep in the Sespe are hope on the hoof.

Though native to the Transverse Ranges, bighorn sheep (*Ovis canadensis nelsoni*) were extinct here by about 1914 owing to a combination of meat and trophy hunting and diseases transferred from domestic livestock. In 1985, however, the California Department of Fish and Game transplanted to the Sespe sheep from a stable population in the San Gabriel Mountains. The transplant didn't go entirely as planned. High winds hampered the helicopters, and the animals touched down over a wide area. They panicked and scattered. Some headed north and disappeared altogether. There were falls from cliffs. I've heard tales of sheep impaled on spearlike branches. Since the sheep were unfamiliar with the steep, rocky escape habitat they depend on, some were picked off by mountain lions. Still, of the thirty-seven that were transplanted, some survived.

By the late '80s, the population appeared to be somewhat stable. New lambs were born, and the sheep had begun to disperse into new habitat. Most, however, stayed in the area where they were dropped, a testament both to the cautious nature of sheep and to habitat assessments that had identified the areas most likely to support sheep. By the early '90s, things had shifted. Biologists had a much harder time finding sheep in the Sespe. The radio collars stopped working or the sheep wearing them died. The last official survey turned up only two sheep, and the DFG decided to end their management work. In the meantime, the sheep population elsewhere in California began to plummet, making further transplants to the Sespe impossible. In the San Gabriels, for example, the population of seven hundred dropped to only thirty-five, below the borderline of what most biologists would consider a viable number for long-term sustainability (McCarty and Bailey 11). The Sespe sheep were on their own.

Recently, after nearly a decade under the radar, the Sespe sheep have staged a miraculous comeback. Actually, they may have been doing fine all along and we humans just didn't notice. It's hard to know. But in late 1999 hunters and hikers started to report sheep sightings. About that same time, on a Sespe adventure, I stepped in my first clue that there were sheep in the Sespe. A raven cronked to let me know the joke was on me. Luckily there was enough untrammeled monkey puzzle scat left to identify. Unmistakably sheep, but at the time it was a provocative mystery. I had seen no sheep and had heard no mention of sheep. Yet here was evidence of things not seen.

A year later I decided to get serious about confirming my faith. I made some calls to the Department of Fish and Game, and the kind biologists there told me the whole story. When they seemed sure I was not a trophy hunter, they suggested that I might have a chance to see sheep right where I had stepped in the evidence a year earlier. I planned a midweek hike when I might get the canyon to myself. I started out early on my path to the bighorns' "escape habitat" and to my own.

From a few hundred yards across the canyon, I watch the ewe browse her way down the cliff above the source of a hot spring. Every couple of minutes she looks straight off the cliff for a few moments, but I can't figure out what she's looking at or for. Near the springs she switches from mountain mahogany to the mineral-rich grass growing on the banks of the hot creek. After a few minutes she crosses the water and joins two other ewes I hadn't noticed. Together the three make their way slowly along the creek. One stands in the open spot where I pitched a tent on my first visit eight years ago. Another crosses the creek on the rock sieve that forms a pool I've soaked in many times. Since I haven't had a good rear view of the two new ewes, I pull out my cheat sheet with pictures distinguishing yearling rams from mature ewes. I look again at the sheep, and all three are staring directly at me. I may as well have waved my arms as flash the 8½ by 11 photocopy.

Gradually, they graze again, slowly making their way up a rocky slope. One of them always has an eye on me. I've watched for almost an hour. I put on my pack, walk down along the ridge, filter water from the cold creek in the other canyon, then walk up to where I'll camp near a good soak pool. The sheep are a couple hundred yards up the slope above my camp, so I kick back and watch them through binoculars. A non-native palm thicket shields most of my activity, and the ewes seem aware of me but relaxed.

Then the drama starts. I stand to get my lunch from my pack and a shape catches my eye through the brush. A gorgeous, full-curl, class IV ram stands near the creek at my level watching the ewes intently. He starts up toward them and doesn't stop to graze on the way. I look back to the ewes. They betray no awareness of the ram and continue grazing. The ram reaches the first ewe and gives a butt-sniff greeting while the other two now watch closely from a rock outcropping above. He makes the rounds but doesn't seem too welcome. For a time they all graze together, and I take the opportunity to duck behind the palm windbreak to inflate my sleeping pad and stuff it into my camp-chair frame. I watch the sheep as I step from behind the windbreak with the bright blue chair. The ewes don't react, but the ram goes rigid. I realize he's been so distracted he hasn't seen me before, even though I've been in plain sight the whole time, writing, munching, and restlessly shifting positions. He stares right at me for a few minutes while the females fan out and continue eating. By this time, the ewes have known about me for two and a half hours. Finally, the ram walks over to the nearest ewe and resumes sampling her urine. One of the ewes, who has drifted away behind a boulder pile, appears suddenly and startles the rest. They take two leaps up the nearest steep rock, pause, look around, and graze again.

The ram begins to herd the females together. He backs one of them toward a vertical cliff face. She retreats until she's cornered, then in a quick move darts around the ram and joins the others. He tries for others with similar results. I hear the delayed crackle of rockfall as they leap and scamper.

During the next hour the ram's courtship behavior gradually becomes more aggressive. He picks one out, and together they move in tight circles around the others. He kicks out with his forelegs occasionally. He fakes right and goes left to get himself in a position to mount, but the second his front hooves leave the ground she slips away. He tries again, fails again. He moves on to the next female. I find it hard to correlate much of what I'm seeing with the textbook courtship descriptions emphasizing interactions between rams. I've got only one, but I'm rooting for him. This has nothing to do with male partisanship. I just want more sheep for the Sespe.

At 2:30 P.M. the sun has already left the bottom of the canyon, but on the ridge the ewes lie down and soak up its warmth. I decide to make my long-delayed lunch and set up camp. I'm curious to know if my moving around will disturb the sheep. It's a little ironic that in this wilderness so seemingly spacious to human eyes, the sheep have gathered in the place most likely to see human traffic. Before 1978 when the Forest Service declared the Sespe "roadless," it was possible to skid a motorbike down Johnston Ridge or four-wheel through stream crossings on a now-vanished road running east from Lion Camp. A friend told me about the time that he had hiked with a few others seventeen miles from Lion Camp to the hot springs. They set up tents in the quiet just as a beat-up van bounced over the rocks and came to a dusty, fumy halt. A guy leaned through the open window to inquire, "You guys know where I can score some acid?"

Today, this is official wilderness, and you have to walk. Plenty of folks do, inspired by the hot springs, which can be approached from three directions. I was told that on the millennial New Year's Eve there were over thirty people crowding around the springs, which seem to function as the regional spiritual center. Vulvic drawings scraped into the tufa near the 180-degree source suggest some think of the spring in terms of mythic sexuality. In the upper reaches of the canyon you can find faux pictographs that look like someone's version of aliens. And in the center of a labyrinth marked out in stones, the meditative have left shells, beads, and necklaces. Sometimes I find stone cairns balanced with precarious and unnatural precision.

Because of all this human activity—and my own presence—I'm curious to know whether and how humans affect the sheep. The biologists I've talked to don't seem particularly worried so long as there is no obvious and deliberate harassment. But since it would be very difficult to keep people out of this canyon, I wonder whether their opinions are partly a practical concession to the realities of mixed-use land management. Research on the responses of sheep to humans raises questions about even seemingly benign interactions. During the 1970s and '80s the opinion was mixed on the effects of human intrusion. In the San Gabriel Mountains, habitat abandonment correlated with the movement of sheep to avoid humans. However, other researchers concluded that small numbers of humans on foot or horseback were not necessarily detrimental, although sheep seemed to react more to people on foot than to moving vehicles and aircraft. More recently, Craig McCarty and James A. Bailey have questioned the assumptions of earlier researchers about the relationship between sheep movement and contact with humans (13). They point out that avoidance depends on available habitat. If there is no place to go or if resources are scarce, the lack of avoidance may indicate elevated negative stress levels. A sheep seeming to stand calmly for good photos may in fact be a bundle of nerves. Researchers monitoring the heart rates of disturbed sheep have confirmed that outwardly calm sheep sometimes register significant anxiety. Since a stressed sheep expends more energy, and its depressed immune system increases its risk of disease, the sheep in marginal habitat frequented by people has compounding problems in its quest to survive and pass on genes.

I think of how the startled ram cut short his courtship behavior for ten minutes to stare at me. His heart rate must have been off the charts. How long did the stress last? Did it affect the way he pursued the three ewes or whether he was successful? It's hard to know. One question I have is whether my solitary presence midweek is more stressful to the sheep than the weekend traffic they may have come to expect. Do the sheep adjust their patterns of movement to the regularity of human intrusion at the hot springs and along commonly used trails? The movements of people in the canyon are probably quite predictable—walk in, soak, eat, soak, drink, soak, sleep, soak, walk out—and the terrain doesn't encourage off-trail hiking. Furthermore, the escape cliff above the spring may allow the sheep to feel secure and to avoid people when they choose without giving up good habitat entirely.

By the time I finish eating lunch, the ram has the three ewes up and in avoidance mode again. They're so busy, it's easy to think they have far too much going on to worry about me. Besides, I'm far below their safe positions high in rocky escape habitat. I couldn't move a step without being in clear view. By the time I eat supper a few hours later, their courtship antics have followed the sun up a notch leading toward the top of the cliff.

When it grows too dark for me to see even their white butts, I strip off layers of synthetic fleece and stand in the bracing wind before slipping into the nearest hot pool. Eyes shut, I absorb the heat and breathe the night chill deeply. I run my hands over the algae-slick rocks. Heat up, rinse off, give thanks. The stars accumulate. Holding my hands up to dry, I put on my head lamp, lean back at just the right cant to relieve the pebble pressure on my rump, and open Wallace

Stegner's *Angle of Repose.* The book had provided a packing dilemma, since I had finished 250 pages and wasn't about to rip the book apart to save weight. But none of the lighter unread books on my shelf inspired, and now it's just the right thing to read of folks making a difficult home of the West.

Still thrilled as I was with seeing the sheep, the whole scene feels almost too sensuous and luxurious. I lack only a good piece of chocolate or some cookies for dessert. I'll have to make do later with my little airplane bottle of tequila. I sit up from my reclining rock to cool off in the up-canyon breeze. The creek's effervescent tingle curves around my back and eddies by my belly and under my arms. I turn the headlamp off, place the book in the grass on the bank, and adjust my eyes to the night. I think of the sheep on the ridge and wonder how many other Sespe ridges hold and hide beasts breathing evenly until morning.

Nearly a year later, two years after I first stepped in sheep scat, I'm filling out a liability form and statement of loyalty to the U.S. Constitution in the meeting room at the Chuchupate Ranger Station in Frazier Park. I'm to be part of the ground crew for the optimistically named First Annual Upper Sespe Bighorn Sheep Count. Gradually, the room fills up with DFG and USFS personnel, members of the Society for the Protection of Bighorn Sheep, other professors and a couple of students, and folks who like wilderness. Groups of us will head out tomorrow to observation points. At dawn the following morning we'll look for sheep as a helicopter full of biologists flies over areas inaccessible by human foot. The organizers seem flexible, so I'm allowed to switch groups to go up San Rafael Peak and through an area I've never seen before. As the groups gather around topo maps spread on the floor, the excitement seems to build. We follow the trails, count contour lines, and discuss off-trail routes. We're imaginative people about to begin an adventure.

Later, I zone out as a helicopter pilot goes over the radio protocol—emergency frequencies, fire procedures, relays and repeaters. It all mixes together, and I decide I had better avoid using a radio for fear of causing communication chaos. I can never understand the electrified voices over walkie-talkies anyway and just waste batteries asking for repeats, or worse, asking what the code is for a repeat. The slide program is more entertaining. We see examples of the wide horn base that indicates a yearling ram rather than a ewe. We discuss whether the tips of a ram's horns are splintered enough to nudge it from class III into class IV. Everyone calls out different numbers as we try to count the sheep in a slide. At the end of the orientation I'm handed a radio and a heavy spare battery. I try to demure, considering not only my radio idiocy but also the weight. I'll be carrying six liters of water up a mountain in addition to the rest of my gear, and I don't want to add to the mass. But they insist, and I stuff them into my pack.

A year before this official count, the DFG did a preliminary helicopter count that turned up twenty-nine animals. Given that such counts typically sight one-third of the population, the presumed numbers— perhaps ninety—were enough to warrant further investigation. Ninety, however, is still a precarious number. Valdez and Krausman refer to a study that found that all herds of fewer than fifty animals became extinct within seventy years, while all herds with more than a hundred individuals persisted for more than seventy years (247). To give the Sespe sheep a boost toward long-term viability, the DFG decided the next step was to gather existing research and begin to do habitat assessment. Thanks to Geographic Information Systems software, habitat attributes such as foraging patches, corridors, and escape habitat can be quantified and modeled with more specificity than when the sheep were originally transplanted. GIS allows biologists to simulate changes to habitat quality under various management schemes. The ultimate goal, of course, will be to put it all together and come up with a management plan to help out the sheep that have survived the decade by themselves.

While it might be tempting to think that if the sheep have survived for this long without help, they can continue to thrive without intervention, this view fails to recognize the degree to which humans already influence changes in even isolated ecosystems. In other locations, sheep have been particularly sensitive barometers of the unintentional effects of human actions. Recent research in the Wind River Range in Wyoming, for example, traces plunging sheep populations to selenium deficiencies in vegetation caused by acid rain (Polakovic). When the rain leaches the crucial mineral from their food, lambs born healthy sicken and die within weeks of birth. At the same time, ewes leave escape habitat and risk predation to seek out the mineral. Kills by lions and other predators rise as the survival rate of lambs falls.

California provides another example of how humans affect sheep populations from afar. In 1990, a ballot initiative passed that banned all killing of mountain lions by hunters and even wildlife managers except in extreme circumstances. At the time, the law seemed to make sense to environmentalists who saw the hunting of lions with packs of dogs as a cruel vestige of a frontier history that we've evolved beyond. When the inevitable increase in lion populations corresponded with a fall in the numbers of deer, their primary prey, lions began to kill more sheep. Previously stable populations in the Sierra Nevada have been decimated as a result. Sheep that survived were found to alter their foraging habitats in response to the threat of lions. In turn, poor nutrition generally yields lower birth rates and higher mortality during the winter.

In the Sespe, biologists still don't know the precise effects of lion predation or other factors. They're focusing more on the fundamentals: sheep need habitat, and increasing that habitat can only help. But this is not a simple matter.

A classic study of mountain sheep conducted by Valerius Geist in British Columbia in the 1960s explains some of the complexities. Geist found that sheep depend on knowledge of home ranges and seem to pass that knowledge along in ways that could be described as cultural. Geist writes, "Young sheep that follow adults adopt the habits of older individuals, habits which have been proved successful for generations and which allowed the leaders to grow old" (126). In undisturbed wilderness areas, he found that sheep would move between patches of habitat predictably. Persistent disturbance—hunting, for example, or recreational traffic—can result in juveniles losing contact with adults and wandering on their own. Survival rates in such cases decline. If corridors are closed off and patches of habitat are lost, sheep have difficulty incorporating distant patches into their home ranges because they are hesitant to strike out through unknown territory that takes them away from known escape habitat and makes them easy targets for predators.

In the Sespe, one can easily see how this dynamic might work. Slopes ideal for sheep—those punctuated by single shrubs and grasses and broken up by steep, rocky faces—are most often islands in vast seas of chaparral. Line of sight, the primary defense for sheep, becomes useless once they leave these islands. While deer seem willing to move through the brush on trails also used by bears, coyotes, and lions, bighorn sheep do not. I know how they feel. Trying to make one's way through a decades-old forest of brush can be profoundly claustrophobic. I've never seen a lion in the Sespe, but I've seen tracks many times, and I've felt the hair on the back of my neck stand up while hiking alone through thick cover.

It's too early to know what the DFG management plan will consist of, but it seems likely that the isolated patches of foraging and escape habitat could be linked by reintroducing a crucial element of chaparral ecology—fire. Much of the Sespe—like much of Southern California—has not burned in decades. The chaparral has reached a climax stage dominated by scrub oak and chamise, which is sometimes called greasewood for its incendiary qualities. Controlled burns in climax chaparral can be dicey enterprises, since the capacity for massive, devastating fires grows as the fuel loads accumulate over vast areas. The irony, of course, is that such fuel loads are at once the result of decades of fire suppression and the justification for continued suppression.

Fire suppression in Southern California dates back to 1793 when the governor of Upper and Lower California, Don José Joaquín de Arrillaga, banned the native practice of burning grasslands (Timbrook, Johnson, and Earle 130). The Spanish, who saw the grasslands as pasture for livestock, failed to perceive that native Californians regularly set fires to stimulate the growth of seed plants and edible bulbs and shoots. Spanish accounts and ethnographic records indicate that the Chumash burned coastal grasslands regularly, but it's less clear whether this practice extended into the chaparral hillsides and inland areas. While it is possible that burns in chaparral started through escaped lowland burns and campfires or lightning strikes, some argue that indigenous people were maintaining chaparral belts and were "active, selective agents in the very evolution of California's chaparral" (Lewis 94). In any case, it is clear that fire, now largely suppressed for over two hundred years, drives the dynamic, cyclical nature of chaparral ecology. In its absence, bighorn sheep habitat shrinks.

But mentioning fire in Southern California is like opening Pandora's box. Most people who have lived here for a while have personal stories of walls of smoke and flame, even if they and their property have not been directly threatened. It seems to go without saying that fires should be put out as they start, for even fires in remote regions could ride Santa Ana winds to threaten homes within hours. Here as elsewhere, fire fighting is seen as noble and heroic, a classic struggle against the brute force of malevolent nature. This is especially true since the summer of 2000, when "controlled" burns nearly wiped out Los Alamos, New Mexico, and fires raged throughout the West. Interestingly, these events have sparked publicity about the ecological benefits of burning and have led some to question the wisdom of building neighborhoods in picturesque forests. Nevertheless, the culture of fire fighting is entrenched. After the summer of 2000, the U.S Congress provided $1.9 billion to fund fire fighting, and although the summer of 2001 saw only one-fourth the number of acres burn, the U.S. Forest Service still ran up a $230 million cost overrun ("Costly" 11).

However, the political climate is not the only factor for bighorn biologists considering the use of fire. A controlled burn gone wrong could also threaten the sheep directly, despite the best intentions. Clearly, the Sespe sheep do not have the numbers to withstand such losses. On the other hand, it could also be argued that small burns, done right, lessen the chances of a large-scale fire sending the whole herd up in smoke. Hopefully, careful burn prescriptions, accurate weather forecasts, and precise control of the helitorches will allow for the harnessing of a potentially wild management tool.

Yesterday we reached the summit of San Rafael Peak by evening. Under a small cairn I found a tin can containing two small notebooks bearing the signatures of hikers all the way back to the mid-1980s.

Flipping the pages, I could chart the annual visits of biologists keeping track of the transplanted bighorns until 92 when they found none and gave up. I recognized the names of two men in a group of Sierra Club twenties and thirties singles. Interesting strategy, I thought—those guys are easily in their forties and fifties. Then I noticed the date—1985. Most of the signatures were from "peak baggers," who hunt down mountains and count them like trophies. They write the number of peaks they've bagged in a little outline of mountains. A satirical spirit signed "Ursus Schwartz." In a little outline of mountains, Schwartz wrote, "1, for the 723rd time—stay the hell off my mountain!" Some humorless, monolingual peak bagger responded, "Go to hell!" When I put the notebooks back into the tin and stash it under rocks, the mountain seemed more peaceful.

Now, before dawn, on a ridge just below the peak, I've found a flat, smooth rock perfect for comfortable observation. Sitting up and facing southeast I can rest my elbows on my knees to keep the binoculars steady. Lying on my belly with my chin on the rock, I can look into another drainage to the west. In either drainage, I can trace ridgelines for a few miles all the way down to Sespe Creek. For most of the way, the south-facing slopes are relatively open, mountain-size piles of rock veined by a few spring-fed seeps. Here and there the roots of mountain mahogany, scrub oak, and yucca keep things from tumbling down. This is fine habitat for bighorns, and to the east I can see other big pockets of escape terrain on the rocky slopes of McDonald and Cobblestone Peaks. Still, between these pockets grow thick elfin forests of chaparral.

Shortly after first light, I turn my radio on and listen to the rest of my group calling their positions to a coordinator on a nearby mountaintop. I press the button to talk and the battery dies. I try the other battery. Dead. I give thanks and turn to the business of finding sheep. But I find everything other than bighorn sheep. Shrubs, shadows, and stones. Many, many stones. Still, I diligently scan the slopes. I try to remember the hunter's advice articles I read in *Outdoor Life* when I was twelve, but all I come up with is to look for horizontal lines to spot deer in a forest. That's no help at all here in this world of multipoint perspective, intersecting rock planes, shifting light, and subtle shading. Training in cubist painting might help. After a couple of hours, I wave as the helicopter flies over signaling the end of my shift. For me it's a bust, but that doesn't matter. I believe the bighorns are out there somewhere. Later, I find out that the crew down by the hot springs sees nearly twenty sheep, including lambs. Maybe the lambs indicate the courtship I watched eleven months earlier was ultimately successful. Go sheep!

The sun warms the top of the mountain, and I stuff my long johns, hat, and gloves into my pack and look down the mountain toward the trailhead. I'll follow a ridge down the north slope—different from the way up. I'll meet the trail along the creek, then climb up and over the saddle and through the ponderosa forest at the edge of a sagebrush and lupine pasture. I'll dust myself off at the truck and put on a clean T-shirt before driving out along the dirt road that leads to the twisting paved road through Lockwood Valley. I'll drop off the dead radio at Chuchupate Ranger Station and stop in Frazier Park for something other than water to drink—something with fizz. I'll put on a CD when I get to Interstate 5, and the music should last the rest of the drive home. The whole trip should take about five hours, but part of me will stay up here on the mountain. We all need escape habitat of one sort or another.

CHAPTER 3

Bear in Mind

Shadows of the California Grizzly

*The end of the bear as a physical presence coincides with the end of
a human way of being at peace on the earth. The lack of bears and
human disillusion are not merely coincidental.*

—PAUL SHEPARD, *Encounters With Nature*

Waiting in meadows for condors on the wing or among the rocks for
bighorn sheep, I've tried to imagine the Sespe from the point of view
of beings different from me. By learning their ways, I've tried to give
myself up to their world, this world, knowing all the while that my
transformations will be only partial and imaginative. It shouldn't surprise me that the more I lose myself to these creatures, the more I find
within what seems true and fitting. My empathy would begin to grow
after I had read about them and talked with biologists, then my heart
would leap when I saw the turning speck in the sky or heard the clat-
ter of hooves on stone. I wonder, though, what it would mean to try
to see the Sespe through the eyes of a creature that no longer exists
and cannot appear before me in such timely fashion as the condors
and bighorns. This would be a different test of the imagination and of
a peculiar sort of memory.

Case in point: there used to be grizzly bears in the Sespe, and now that they are gone the place is diminished. So often now, we must come to terms with a place by delving into its loss. Yet it's not that simple. There are still bears in the Sespe Wilderness, just not grizzlies. A healthy number of black bears have moved in and made themselves at home in the wake of the grizzly's extinction. To feel this as a loss is, I suppose, prejudicial to black bears.

Perhaps it would be better to describe the shift from grizzlies to black bears as a change—or, more evocatively, as a transformation. A lost species is irrecoverable and a break with the future. The ideas of change and transformation might, however, help us move with hope into the future even where the past contains a measure of loss. In other words, we can't bring back the California grizzlies, but we can remember them as we attend to the place and to the life that remains. These considerations are not entirely abstract for me, for I've found that I can better contemplate what is absent from the Sespe when I am away from it, sitting at home surrounded by books. When I feel rocks rolling under my boots or when the brush rustles as I pass, the overwhelming present remains sufficient to restore me even if it has been diminished. When I look at a trail where my own footprints mix with those of a bear, any kind of bear, my heart and belly let me know that the place is working on—and into—me. In that moment my self swells and shrinks all at once.

You can see I'm trying to resolve a paradox confronting all who find rejuvenation in what we call "nature." How do we reconcile our unbounded joy in a present place with the endless stream of bad news from the front lines? How can we take such pleasure when the last, best places are nothing like they were? Well, in the Sespe backcountry the pleasure comes easily. Compared with much of Southern California, the Sespe appears pristine; it still presents the mystery and energy to satisfy spiritual longing and intellectual curiosity. Its wildness allows us to repress knowledge of the parade of extinction and the chemicals drifting in from the Los Angeles Basin. This is good. In small, homeopathic doses, such repression keeps us healthy. I partake regularly, though I know I will find the whole—if unsettling—truth more satisfying. Even as beauty leaves me speechless and thankful, I tell myself that dimension and depth lie beneath shimmering surfaces and that stories of the past might enliven the present.

Sometime after 1912, a very old Chumash man by the name of Fernando Librado Kitsepawit spoke with the ethnographer J. P. Harrington about some of the last of the bear-men, who could see the world as the bears did. The story begins with Ustaquio, an old Ventura vaquero. When he was young, Ustaquio found a bearskin suit on Sisa, a mountain near the town of Ojai. Such a suit was worn by bear-men, and it was complicated. The skin-wearer would have killed a bear, skinned it carefully in one piece, then stuffed it with grass to mimic the bulk of a real bear. Perhaps the man would have placed pitch in the nostrils, leaving the nose a bit runny. Or he may have cleared one nostril through which to grunt. A piece of abalone shell would have given the tongue a glistening appearance. For the truest effects, he would have suspended small baskets of water under the arms to resemble the sloshing innards of a real bear and carried a basket of crushed manzanita berries to drop occasionally along his way. Inside the skin were three looped cords for the fingers to pull. A bear-man would know that the index finger was for walking, the middle for running, and the ring finger for turning.

Ustaquio, however, was not a bear-man; he was just fooling around, and when he put on the skin, he couldn't control it. He set off running and couldn't stop until he bumped into Nordhoff Ridge, above Ojai. Quickly, he took the skin off and returned it to the cave where a bear-man had hidden it. Moving through the Sespe as a bear apparently took practice, maybe an apprenticeship. It wasn't something just anyone could do, even with the right equipment.

Another story, though, suggests why Ustaquio may have been curious about bear-suits, for his father was a bear-man. One night Ustaquio was carousing with his fellow vaqueros when they roped a bear. They quickly saw that it was not a real bear by the way it removed the rope with two paws. A real bear used one. Yet Ustaquio, who had taken a vow after being injured by a bear to kill all bears, charged this one with a sword: "As he began a third onslaught the bear spoke and said, 'My son!, don't kill me! I forgive you, for I am at fault.

I forgive you all, for people are doing away with bears'" (Blackburn 259). The other vaqueros help convince Ustaquio to spare his father's life, and they carry the old man back to Ventura, where he dies soon after.

At the heart of this story, the father's cry of forgiveness, tangled with grief, transforms the building tension and leaves me wondering at its depth. "My son!" Offering absolution in the absence of repentance, the father bears the burden of his tormenters' arrogance and fear. His words are gratuitous, forming a hole in the story into which my understanding tumbles. The unreasonable grace removes any hope for an appropriate justice and throws the story and me off balance. And rightly so, since for the father and the son, and for me, the world is off-kilter; only the father seems to acknowledge this and accept his part in the loss.

I can only guess at the feeling behind the father's words. Though old, he may have lived his whole life since the coming of the Spanish to the Southern California coast and the establishment of the missions. After the missions, he lived into the period of the large ranchos created through Spanish and Mexican land grants. He was still a bearman, however, a keeper of traditional Chumash knowledge about relationships between the physical and spiritual worlds. The survival of such knowledge through the generations since the Spanish invasion to the time of the story is in itself remarkable, though the practices of a bear-man would have been private and secretive and, like the last of the grizzlies hiding out in the deepest chaparral, persistent beyond expectation. But survival would not have been easy, and the father seems to know he's at the end of the line figuratively as well as literally. As one of the last of this sort of mediator between human beings and animals—that is, as one whose responsibility was to maintain the larger community—he may have felt he had failed. He seems able to imagine only the loss inherent to change. Crucially, he expresses these emotions through his tie to another species: "for people are doing away with bears."

It is likely that he contemplated his failings for years, as all around him bears were being killed. He must also have known the risk of moving over the landscape as a bear. Although he accepted the risk, one can sense his humiliation on being dragged out of the brush at the end of *la riata* (lariat) by his own son. As with so many conflicts between generations, the two figures represent different responses to a changing world. The son, like many Chumash men, went to work as a vaquero for the ranchos. Ustaquio knew that times had changed, and with the flexibility of youth he made his way successfully in the new world. His horse wore a Mexican-style tooled leather saddle. He wore leather *chapparos* to protect himself from the thick coastal brush known as chaparral. He took his oaths in the language and sanctuary of a new religion. The son may have been impatient with the old ways of his father. His embarrassment and need to prove himself and his skills to his *compadres* may have spurred his aggression. We don't know what Ustaquio believed about this cultural shift, but he may have been thinking what another vaquero told a roped bear-man before releasing him: "Tell your friends who do this sort of thing never to dress as bears again. For you people are to blame for a great deal of our suffering and for the fact that we cannot carry out the doctrines taught by the priests. You must promise that neither you nor your friends will do this again. You must not use your herbs" (Blackburn 261). We should remember, however, that it must have been Ustaquio who preserved the voice of his father, telling the story in his old age. By this time the five remaining bear-men would have died and maybe all the grizzlies as well.

This past spring I hiked alone north from Dough Flat on a Monday after a stormy weekend. The surrounding mountains were covered with snow higher up, and heavy rains had made the trail a clean slate of clay marked with the prints of critters. I followed the path of a bobcat for a half mile until it meandered among the handlike raccoon prints in the sand flats along a creek and disappeared under a chamise bush on the bank. As I walked among tracks of rodents and birds, I noticed coyote prints—the old trickster was going along as always. But it was the black bear tracks that stopped me in mine. They were perfect impressions in clay heading up the path I was heading down and ending right where I stood. They didn't seem to angle off or purchase for a leap. They simply stopped as if the bear had vaporized.

Maybe a better tracker could have figured this out. The brush on both sides of the trail seemed too thick for a bear to get through easily, but nevertheless I bent down to the more open underlayer and peered into the thicket for furry legs. I couldn't tell, after all, whether the tracks were thirty seconds or two days old. Clay holds up well.

Over the next couple of days I became accustomed to the idea of bears. Their prints and droppings marked every trail, yet I slept soundly near a creek whose burbling covered twig snaps in the night. After a while it became clear that I saw no bears only because they chose not to be seen. The presence of the bears, even unseen—or rather especially unseen—made the place seem wilder. But I thought often of how even this wildness was diminished. I'd heard enough tales of black bear mayhem to be wary and careful with my food, but I had to admit that my heart would have been beating faster if the tracks were made by grizzlies.

The habitat for grizzlies in Southern California was among the best in the world. But to understand this we need to imagine a landscape different from what we see today. We must imagine vigorous steelhead runs in the Ventura River and its tributary Matilija Creek, the Santa Clara River and its tributary Sespe Creek, and in all the other streams from Monterey to Baja California. Thousands of fish, fattened from the ocean, pool near the mouths of the rivers waiting for spring freshets before dashing upstream to gravel spawning beds in the mountains. We must imagine bighorn sheep scattering rocks on the faces of cliffs. From large herds of antelope and deer the very young, very old, the sick and the injured supplement the bear staples of acorns and berries in the fall and the tender shoots of new plants in spring. We must picture grizzlies grazing in meadows kept free from chaparral by frequent fires set intentionally and carefully by people who have lived here long enough to weave stories from the landscape. On the beaches, the stench of decaying whales and sea lions would draw bears to the feast from miles around. In the mind's eye we glimpse bear heaven.

The arrival of the Spanish in Southern California dramatically changed not only the relationship between people and bears but also the ecology and habitat of bears. The most dramatic changes resulted from the introduction of livestock: Mr. and Mrs. Griz, meet Mr. and Mrs. Bovine, who have long been bred for fat, slowness, and stupidity. In 1854 Raphael Reyes and his brothers drove two thousand head of cattle from Los Angeles to the Cuyama Valley northwest of the Sespe region. In other words, they drove the cattle through and into what was already prime grizzly habitat. With the influx of cattle and the stray horses that bred so effectively that they had to be regularly exterminated, the grizzlies were blessed with more free food than they knew what to do with. The bears even seemed to adopt new hunting techniques to kill cattle. Grizzlies were observed rolling and tumbling and acting crazy in meadows until the dim-witted cattle approached close enough for the bear to bite into a cow's nose, flip it on its side, and rip open its throat (Storer and Tevis 122). In Ojai Valley in 1868, a man named Thomas Clark watched three bears work in concert. One bear balled itself up and came "bounding along like a football rolling toward the cattle, which instead of fleeing, pricked up their ears and watched the strange spectacle" (123). Meanwhile, two other bears attacked the herd unseen from the flanks. One can't imagine antelope or deer falling for this. Sometimes, however, the bears didn't even need to put in any thought or work to gain good meals. Stray horses were such a problem that vaqueros would control herd size by driving horses off cliffs until only a pile of carcasses remained for bears to scavenge (129). In another management technique, an estimated seven to eight thousand horses were driven into the sea at Santa Barbara in 1807 (129). Bears accustomed to finding dead whales and sea lions on the beach had no trouble adding this new flotsam to their diets. Drought also took its toll on stock, with as many as forty thousand horses and cows perishing in the twenty-two months between rains in 1828 and 1830. Grizzlies have always been fond of carrion. In response to increased caloric intake, the grizzly population grew dramatically (26). Raphael Reyes's brother-in-law, Ramón Ortega, *mayordomo* of Rancho Sespe, claimed to have counted a hundred grizzlies between Mission San Buenaventura and the rancho (25). By most accounts, Ortega was a good storyteller, which is to say he was an entertaining liar, but many others claimed similarly frequent sightings throughout Southern California. The grizzly population's most dramatic decrease may have occurred around 1863–64, when drought ended the era of the ranchos and the work of American hunters began to have an effect (128). Ironically, it is through the records and stories of bear killing that we get a sense of the astounding numbers of bears in the region.

Storer and Tevis gathered the records for their 1955 study of the California grizzly (*Ursus arctos californicus*) (25ff.). George Nidever killed forty-five and injured others in what is now San Luis Obispo County in 1837. Colin Preston is said to have killed about two hundred in the central coast region in the 1840s. General Frémont reported killing twelve in a single thicket in San Luis Obispo Valley. Three hunters in the Tejon Pass killed one hundred fifty in 1854. These areas surround the Sespe. Records from the Sespe itself date from the 1870s, as transportation routes through the backcountry opened up. Storer and Tevis suggest that the greatest decline in numbers occurred between 1849 and 1870 (26). These dates correspond to the American occupation of Alta California and some of the most brutal times for the indigenous people of the state as well. As the American population of California increased, bear hunting that had previously taken place mostly near population centers in the valleys moved into the backcountry, with gold miners and ranchers looking for more range. Correspondingly, the bears also moved into the more remote mountainous areas and away from the ecologically rich lowlands they had dominated for centuries (27). Local newspapers recorded many sightings, attacks, and killings in the 1870s, but they reported few killings by the most noted hunters of the area, including Ramón Ortega, though these men may have been taking many (Outland 126). In 1879, one of the best-known hunters, Ari Hopper, namesake of the present-day Hopper Mountain National Wildlife Refuge, reported that grizzlies in the Sespe were extremely scarce (Outland 133).

The area was remote then as now, however, and it is not hard to believe that some of the last surviving local bears could have found refuge in the Sespe backcountry. How long they may have held out is hard to say. There are numerous reports from the 1890s, including the story of a settler from the Sespe Hot Springs area who was coming out over the Last Chance Trail to escape heavy snow. On top of the Topatopa bluffs he saw a grizzly rolling boulders down the mountainside (Outland 143). In 1905, a forest ranger reported tracks, and hunters claimed to have seen a bear in the vicinity of the hot springs and Alder Creek (Outland 144). In the Tejon–San Emigdio high country north of the Sespe, no grizzlies were taken after 1898, the last being killed near Mount Pinos (Storer and Tevis 27). In northern Santa Barbara County, bears were noted as late as 1912. In Los Angeles County the last were shot in the 1890s.

Despite all the hunting, suggests Sespe historian Charles F. Outland, the end of the grizzly came about with a suddenness that can't be explained by hunters, only by strychnine. Hunting and poison, however, may have been only indirectly responsible. This is the way extinction works. Such so-called systematic pressures of humans may reduce a population to the point of rarity. A small population then becomes more vulnerable than a large one to "stochastic perturbations," the chance events that might result directly in the death of the last individuals of a species. In the Sespe around the turn of the nineteenth century, the remaining grizzly population may have been terminally perturbed by any number of things. Maybe it was demographic stochasticity: perhaps ten wily, shy bears—six males, two old females past their reproductive prime, and a sow with a cub—hid out in the thickets until finally an old male killed the cub and gravely wounded the sow. The sow failed to breed again, and gradually, one after the other, they died unnoticed. Maybe it was environmental stochasticity—a disease for instance, or a natural catastrophe such as a fire in prime habitat. Maybe it was a combination of these factors that did in the last bears. Though I have no wish to absolve my own species from responsibility, I find it comforting to imagine that a few bears may have avoided being shot or poisoned and managed to die the way grizzlies ought to die—accident, disease, worn teeth, or intraspecies aggression.

Which brings us back to Ustaquio and his bear-man father. The relative speed of the grizzly's demise in California after a residence of thousands of years provides an essential context for their story. The narrative turns on the loneliness of these words, "people are doing away with bears," spoken by one whose self-conception depends on both people and bears. I hear in the words a "survivor's guilt" based in the loss both of a culture in which the bear-man's transformations have purpose and of the species into which he transformed. Our word "genocide," referring as it does to humans only, seems inadequate to express the completeness of the devastation.

Fernando told more stories about bears and bear-men to Harrington. At La Purisma, young vaqueros killed another bear-man by roping him, dragging him around, and finally stabbing him to death (Blackburn 260). An old Indian from Santa Inez "would turn himself into a bear and pull riatas off when he got lonesome, but he never did any harm" (260). One wonders for whom the old man was lonesome, people or bears? Perhaps the only way he could conscientiously become his bear self was to submit to the misery so common for bears at the time. On the Santa Rita plain, a man roped a bear and asked him what his opinion was of a man on horseback. The bear replied, "Ah, a man on horseback is brave and agile, a thing of power" (261).

Roping bears was great sport among Alta Californians. They would bait the bears and then rope them from highly trained horses, each rider roping a different leg and the neck to pull the bear in different directions (Storer and Tevis 132ff.). Many bears were killed this way, but there were also times when the bears would reel in the horses hand over hand along with their horrified riders. This tended to happen to inexperienced riders and horses.

With regard to the details of bear-roping, the story of Ustaquio's father corroborates the observations of eyewitness accounts. When the old man is roped, he removes the rope with two hands, and the vaqueros see immediately that a real bear would have removed it with the motion of a single paw. This bear behavior corresponds to that recorded in Spanish sources gathered by Storer and Tevis.

It is impossible to know how many California grizzlies occupied the Sespe region and the rest of the Transverse and Coast Ranges prior to the Spanish arrival. They were common, though, and the native human population did not regard them with romantic longing for wildness. Though people occasionally killed grizzlies, the bears generally had little to fear from humans or anything else in their world. They did what they wanted, and they could be dangerous nuisances for indigenous Southern Californians, especially when both were gathering acorns or berries. Early Europeans in the region report many incidents of Native Americans killed by bears or showing the scars from attacks (Storer and Tevis 79).

The Chumash regard for bears as powerful beings is evident in the rock art scattered throughout their homeland. Bears are among the most common representational images in their pictographs. At one site the imprints of carved bear paws emerge when light creates shadow on the sandstone surface. These images may have been created by shamans as records, perhaps even mnemonics, of their visions. Perhaps bear-men saw powerful symbols in bears, whose denning and hibernation could be seen to mimic death and renewed life. Maybe pictographs of bears represent a fascination with an intelligent, instructive animal occupying an ecological niche similar to that of humans. In any case, artistic representation was rooted in direct experience, for bear-men would have spent time away from villages and had the opportunity, at some risk, to observe bears in a natural habitat and to mold their interaction with the world to the habits and manners of bears. Now, as then, the bear's humanlike dexterity and omnivorous versatility sparks human curiosity and imagination:

> It is the bear's broad, searching, persistent openness that makes contact with us, that flash of recognition in which men instantly perceive a fellow being whose questing provocation, whose garrulous, taciturn, lazy ways, even whose obligations to hunt, to hole up, and to dominate the space he lives in are familiar. The bear is a special model of human flexibility, a generalist set against a world of specialists. (Shepard and Sanders 72)

As I attempt to imagine the Sespe as seen through the eyes of those who could see through the eyes of the great bears, I'm helped along by the agile and provocative ideas of the human ecologist Paul Shepard. In *The Others,* Shepard argues that much of what we consider essentially human has evolved through contact with animals. For Shepard, our ability to decipher signs and to order the world categorically stems from our ancestors' careful observations of animals. Animals that didn't fit quite right into single categories encouraged us to come to terms with ambiguity and to think metaphorically. Crucially, a sense of self formed as we assimilated our similarities to and differences from animals. To the poetically inclined, some of Shepard's most compelling support comes in his lists of how our language reveals our appropriation of animal behavior. Fish around a little and you'll find many examples. Bear them in mind.

The implications of Shepard's ideas are shocking if you consider them in the context of our current biodiversity crisis. After all, he says, "No single species could model all the guises needed for the human repertoire. What was required was a reading of ecological diversity as if it were a society" (*The Others* 104). Humans, of course, could then be seen as part of this larger society. If you've already trained yourself to think biocentrically, and if you've come to think of biodiversity as good in and of itself, take a step backward to consider what's in it for you, for us: with the loss of species we may be losing something essential to our humanity. It may be that we can approach the depth of our selves only in relation to a diverse, healthy ecosystem. Without that, we are diminished morally and spiritually.

Elsewhere, Shepard extends still further the implications of his ideas. He suggests that societies that permit and encourage alienation from the natural world are both insane and immature. Without the myths that bind adults to a complex natural world, we are perpetually caught in the throes of adolescence. Maturity, by contrast, would be characterized by "a view broad and forgiving . . . involving a sense of the larger gift of life, a realistic sense of the self and other, and a sense of the talents of generosity and circumspection" (*Nature and Madness* 44–45).

With all this in mind, think back to Ustaquio's story of a conflict between an older man and a group of adolescents. Shepard's use of the phrase "gift of life" helps us to understand the roots of the father's capacity to offer forgiveness, for one response to receiving a gift is to give in return. The gift the father received was the bear and the wisdom of its way of being in the world. Imagine his astonishment that people would so willfully and ignorantly destroy the gift of the grizzly. Yes, grizzlies occasionally must be killed, and he had even killed some himself, but so many so quickly and carelessly? Yet even in his astonishment and growing despair, he tries to act appropriately. His forgiveness attempts to expand the community that participates in the gift. In a beautiful consideration of gift economies, Lewis Hyde writes: "Where we have established such a relationship we tend to respond to nature as a part of ourselves, not as a stranger available for exploitation. Gift exchange brings with it, therefore, a built-in check upon the destruction of its objects; with it we will not destroy nature's renewable wealth except where we also destroy ourselves" (27).

As the father seeks connectedness with what has been given, the son crafts a different sort of power that conforms to a different sort of world. He bends his horse precisely to his will. He learns to make rope into a dangerous weapon. With his adolescent gang, Ustaquio understands a world in which commodities, in this case cows, transform the land into resource and profit.

The loss of the grizzly in the Sespe and California extends beyond the way bears shaped human imagination and relationships to the environment. With the death of the last California grizzly, the world lost a unique genetic code that had evolved in response to conditions—drought, for example—quite different from those in the greater Yellowstone ecosystem, Montana, British Columbia, or Alaska. The absence of the subspecies is all the more troubling given suggestions that isolated grizzly habitat in Yellowstone, Grand Teton, and Glacier National Parks may not be large enough to allow the bears to sustain genetic diversity and avoid cataclysmic disturbances (Grumbine). The parks function essentially as islands, their large animals isolated from genetic immigration. To solve this problem, plans have been developed to reintroduce grizzlies into the Selway-Bitterroot Wilderness of Montana and Idaho, thus creating a corridor between isolated populations. However, property owners who fear federal intrusion under the Endangered Species Act have been outspoken in their opposition, and the U.S. secretary of the interior has announced that the U.S. Fish and Wildlife Service, the agency responsible for endangered species, will not support reintroduction efforts. There are no guarantees the bear will survive in its present habitat.

Seen from both scientific and more obviously metaphorical points of view, the absence of the grizzly from the places I do most of my hiking sets me to thinking about the conceits of a seventeenth-century poet and preacher. To John Donne, our creation from dust and return to dust at death suggested a radical commonality. Who knew what king or queen (or boar or sow) we might now be inhaling? Such an ever present awareness of death was necessary to a fully valued life. "Any man's death diminishes me because I am involved in mankind," says Donne, "and therefore never send to know for whom the bell tolls; it tolls for thee" ("Meditation XVII"). The more I recognize my involvement not only in humankind but also in the larger community of species, the more I meditate on how each loss of life diminishes all the living.

But not all is lost. It's hard to quantify the change in a place that now supports a healthy black bear population instead of grizzlies. At one time, before major habitat disruptions and hunting, the grizzly was seen as the bear of the chaparral and the black bear as the bear of the forest. As the grizzlies were exterminated from the chaparral of the Sespe region and the rest of the Transverse and Coast mountain ranges, black bears moved in. These black bears are not to be confused with the hot-tubbing, cabin-busting population of the San Gabriel Mountains, which was introduced in the 1930s from Yosemite. The Sespe black bears migrated on their own from ranges in the southern Sierra Nevada and the Tehachapi Mountains, but only after the grizzlies were gone. While there were still grizzlies, their territories didn't overlap much.

More than the grizzly, the black bear is adaptable to a variety of habitats. It ranges over most of North America, wherever there are mature forests or, as in the Sespe region, mixed forest and chaparral with little human disturbance. In the foothill borderland between human population centers and the mountains, the relationship between human habits and black bear habitat resembles that which occurred when Spanish ranching contributed to the rise in the numbers of grizzlies. Instead of livestock, the black bears have avocados, which are rich in fat and readily available in orchards ringing the Los Padres National Forest and its wilderness areas. Although bear-human conflicts occasionally happen in the border zones, black bears in the Sespe are not habituated to backpacker food like many bears in the Sierra Nevada. They are generally quite shy. As one hunter told me on the trail, "these bears get shot at once in a while. It makes a difference." In the years since bear hunting season was moved up to early October to coincide with deer season, the average annual take in the Los Padres National Forest has risen from eight to thirty-two (Wehtje). The increase may be because bears are still quite active in early October before gradually becoming less active as autumn progresses. This year on opening day there were still a few bushes of holly-leaved cherry and redberry that hadn't dried up yet. These and the acorns gave the bears a reason to be up and about, and the piles of fresh scat indicated they were.

It may be a long time before we know how increased hunting will affect the black bear population. The Department of Fish and Game has limited its research to "trend studies" rather than exhaustive and expensive population analyses that would involve significant equipment and labor. Because black bears have low reproductive rates, low population sizes, and large territories, understanding a black bear population can take many years (Powell, Zimmerman, and Seaman 4). Since black bears can live to be twenty years old, a population today reflects impacts accumulated from past years. In other words, the effects of increased hunting may not show themselves for some time. Management decisions based on "current" research will always lag behind the population itself.

For now, though, there seem to be plenty of black bears in the Sespe, and as the habitat has changed, so too have ceremonial relationships. When black bears become nuisances and are shot by landowners with permit or by Fish and Game officials, the hides are sometimes given to contemporary Chumash leaders to be used ceremonially.

Near the bottom of Red Reef Canyon, the trail is bootwide and washed out. Mindful that a slip could be the start of a nasty slide, my friend Mike and I step around shrubs growing midtrail and stop to check the topo map. It's obvious that no one has walked this trail in a while, but the map checks out, right down to every hairpin switchback. So we skirt the slides, dive into the chaparral, and struggle up the ridge through decades-old chamise bushes. Wild cucumber vines entwine our feet, buckthorn draws blood, and the thick duff makes every step seem like walking in sand. Feeling guilty—this is my idea and my map after all—I ask Mike whether we should give up before things get any worse. Mike doesn't pause or look back but replies, "Hey, I live for this!" Despite the frustration, I smile and admit to myself that I do too. I decide to take him seriously, and we continue.

But for the vines, the trail remains somewhat clear from the ground to about three feet high where the brush closes in. The only alternative to crawling is to try to gain momentum and blast through. I follow by about fifteen feet to leave room for branches to backlash harmlessly, but I seldom see Mike. Occasionally, I hear huffing sounds at tough spots. I start to think about bears, wondering where they would go off trail to get out of the way of two clumsy, sweaty bipeds.

We keep climbing, fighting greasewood for every step, this time with me in the lead, staring at my feet since there is nowhere else to look and I need to protect the skin on my face. Finally the "trail" opens up a little and we come to a set of mysterious, gorgeous folds in the hills. Red ribs of rock fold down from above and bend toward the creek a few hundred feet below. Pines and juniper cling in the gaps between stone, and up higher we can see stands of big cone spruce, the southern California version of the Douglas fir. The afternoon light has angled enough to shade the opposite side of the canyon and cast a warm sandstone glow around us. Then I look down to see the trail we should be on, unmistakably clear and well traveled, following the creek bed on the other side of the canyon. Not on the map. But the worst of the bushwhacking is over, and I can almost be thankful for the old topo leading us astray into this enchanted place among the rocks. Almost.

Then, as we start to walk again, I look down and notice that my feet fit well in a well-worn path of footprints, only I don't have enough feet to get the rhythm right. It's like stumbling while reading aloud a line of fine poetry. Then it hits me. We're on a bear path, where each bear steps in the prints of the one before it, wearing deep impressions into the soft duff. This is the first bear path I've seen, though I've heard of them. As I look at the perfect regularity of the impressions, I wonder if it takes any attention for each bear to step in the right places or whether the path is simply the result of the natural rhythm of four-footed walking. In either case, to see the trail is to see time compressed: generations of black bears making a home of the Sespe. As we continue, I can see my lug soles are not doing the trail any good, and I feel like an intruder. I hope it doesn't take too many bear trips to repair the damage. More than once I want to lose the pack, drop to all fours, and move through the scrub protected by a thick coat of fur. Glancing back to the trail marked by bear tracks and marred by my own, I think of the stories and poems I know that tell of desire strong enough to pull a person away from his or her people toward the beauty of bears. Sometimes even the pleas of loved ones are not enough to call the person back.

As I step in the prints of black bears, I imagine those of grizzlies beneath layers of soil, generations of growth and decay. The Sespe backcountry has changed, but it is still good. Re-creation is ongoing around and within me. Pausing to lean against pale sandstone, I consider the bear that may be nearby, listening, keeping track of me. I imagine myself in the mind of a bear.

CHAPTER 4

Seeing Through Stone

Visions of Chumash Rock Art

Life is short, the art long. —HIPPOCRATES

By thinking about bears I learned that it's not enough to consider only the land or the creatures that used to live here. It became clear that as ecosystems were altered, so too were minds and cultures. To contemplate an evolving landscape one must see the shifting shapes of human relationship to the place. The Sespe, from what I can tell, was remote and wild even for its first people, though they had the time—centuries—to cultivate deep knowledge and perhaps wisdom in the ways they used it. Yet this longstanding relationship changed suddenly and dramatically. I hope to understand something of how this happened from a few suggestive clues.

And so yesterday, once again, I left my warm bed, drove to a trailhead, and carried my pack a long ways. This morning I unzip the tent at first light to find that the new grass around the old oak bears mid-March frost. The canyon wren's scale descends through the sharp, predawn air, backed by the burbling creek. I'm barely awake, and my mind drifts into the shadows above the creek where a cave protects Chumash pictographs. I've walked a long way with vague directions to see them. Or more precisely, as I considered last night, I've come to be in their presence, to let them work on my imagination, or not. So I've avoided the cave to attend first to its context, hoping delayed gratification will sharpen my perception. Now I lay cultivating the borderline between sleep and wakefulness, night and day, wondering about the shapes I will soon see. I try to recall my dreams, but I've slept like the stone itself.

The evening before, I had stumbled gratefully into this perfect camp. For an hour, I had been walking toward dusk while contemplating having to sleep on the trail beside the creek, a dismal prospect given the piles of bear scat every hundred yards. I didn't wish to make a bear decide whether to turn around or step over my body. But my mind eased as I paused to take in the grassy clearing centered by the ancient oak with a branch the size of a mature tree running fifteen yards parallel to the ground. I leaned my pack against a stone and exchanged my boots for sandals. Knowing it would be cold, I set up my tent and went to the creek to filter water in the dimming light. Then I saw the cave. I simply looked up and it was there, looking down. This must be the place. I turned away and made dinner just as darkness fell.

Now, in the morning, I'm holding myself back again. Better to wait for more light and watch birds over breakfast. Ravens fly by but ignore me. A flicker's wings glow orange swinging toward a big cone spruce up on the ridge. I don't see the quail, but I hear their hoots and wails. A hummingbird flashes—alders in bloom. A scrub jay hangs around camp waiting for me to finish, hoping I'm sloppy. Everything seems right with the world. Everyone knows a fitting place and goes about his business. Then I look up at the sound of a propeller plane on one of the many flight paths above the Sespe backcountry, but I don't see the plane. I see a perfect v of snow geese heading straight north. I blink, and the v explodes as if hit by an air grenade. Geese tumbling in all directions. Urgent honking. Maybe they flew into the wake of the ghost plane. Gradually the v re-forms.

I wonder: Do sights like the tumbling geese appear stranger and more memorable because the pictographs rest in a cave nearby? Will my perceptions of old paintings on stone shift according to the sounds and sights of birds or planes? Will my response be shaped by the creek's timbre? How will my memory turn upon returning with a friend in two months to lower water and higher poison oak, when I know the way and am sure of the destination? Will what I see in the forms have much to do with the pictographs themselves, or will this be just another way of looking at myself? The interplay of images, environment, and my own expectations seems too complex to sort through. Yet I'm left with a sense of overwhelming completeness, or more honestly, a sense that I should be able to feel in the core of my being more of this ultimate integrity. There is always something beyond understanding, something that cannot be articulated. Maybe this absence in the midst of presence is why viewing rock art often feels somewhat anticlimactic.

Since I have doubts about the possibility of knowing "the original meanings" of rock art, I've decided to err on the side of imagination. The research will come later to fuel the fires; now I seek the power in the combination of place and image. Yet as I finish my coffee, I wonder if I may be stalling for a different set of reasons altogether. What if I believe there *is* power associated with the paintings? How might it affect me? Am I intruding and disturbing the peace? If my imagination and desire must inevitably pull these images out of context, why am I here at all?

One author suggests that contemporary fascination with rock art may be a kind of exorcism of colonialism's legacy. She writes, "The victors return to the sites because in some ways the voices of the vanquished are more eloquent than the voices that eclipsed them" (Lippard ix). Yet it is not a simple question to ask what, exactly, is being said by these eloquent voices. How can we be sure that we are not casting our own voices and hearing what we want to hear? Have we mistaken listening for yet another appropriation at a time when we can take what notions we want from this place without fear of reprisal?

Perhaps the wisest move would be to pack up and hike out and not spend another night alone thinking too much in a canyon frequented by bears. Definitely thinking too much. Time to relax, breathe in, breathe out, get up and walk over.

I pass under the oak and cross the creek by leaping to an unstable island of snags. The mountains at the head of the creek's valley hold snow from last week's storms, and the water is high and cold. Beneath the cave I find a subtly placed metal box for visitor registration. It's nestled comfortably in the poison oak. The feeling of remoteness and discovery I've cultivated fades, and the difficulty of the previous day's hike gets put into perspective by the comments of the Boy Scouts here a month before. One fourteen-year-old writes, "It's OK, but I wish there was a TV here and a skatepark." Another says "Good place, but insane cows ate my tent! Ohhh!" No cows in this canyon. Crows maybe? As much as I cherish the solitude, I think it would be a good thing for more fourteen-year-olds to walk this far for such still, silent rewards. But paradoxically, too many appreciative visitors would place the pictographs at risk.

I skirt the footwide sandstone ledge along the cliff twenty feet above the creek and enter the cave, where men and condors merge and people might become bears. Climbing carefully, trying not to raise dust, I lie back on the rock that must have held the painters—a natural platform as effective as the one that held Michelangelo an arm's length from the ceiling of the Sistine Chapel. The spider, outlined in white dots. The polychrome crayfish or lobster, the sections of its fantail clear. The bear-man, arms akimbo. The fringed wings of the condor. The lower half of a frog. Sea animals, graceful as if moving under water. Some shapes have no associations with the world I live in. Dreams and visions take shape before my waking eyes.

The survival of pictographs into the present is surprising, given their vulnerability. Water seeping along the cave wall may dilute the pigments, or the stone may flake, taking with it portions of images. Too often, images bear scars of deliberate violence, such as scraped initials or bullet chips. Even unintentional acts can damage the paintings—oil from a too-curious finger will deteriorate the pigments; dust raised by too-quick feet will fade them; soot from a nearby fire will smudge them. Given the fragility of backcountry rock art sites, I don't encourage anyone to seek them out, especially by trying to follow my vague, perhaps misleading descriptions. Well-known sites like Painted Cave in the mountains above Santa Barbara are easily accessible, well protected, and contain pictographs in many ways more varied and remarkable than those in most backcountry sites.

Perhaps this vulnerability is part of what leads so many researchers and interpreters to view rock art sites as precious windows to an almost irrecoverable past. I sense in rock art scholarship—in the site numbers and figure lists—a touch of the "salvage" impulse that led nineteenth-century ethnographers to fan out across the continent to "collect" the stories of people who were assumed to be dying off. Written down in ethnographers' notebooks and published in collections, versions of stories that once had breathed and changed with the needs of the tellers and the hearers became authoritative and static. Interpreters continue to argue in print about the meanings of the stories, applying the latest theories to attempt understanding of the cultures behind the stories. I've even tried this myself, though I was lucky enough to be working with trickster stories, which always keep moving and doubling back on you, even in print. And paintings on stone, cataloged and given identification numbers, remarkable in their survival, seem even more stable than words on a page. We look at the images and think we might be able to know just enough to solve some of their enigmas.

It is our nature to make meaning from signs, our own or those of others. We can't help it. If the tips of fingers or brushes, mixing pigment and pressed to stone, and the tips of tongues, curling breath into words and stories, give shape to a shifting universe, so too does the viewing and the hearing. The experience of meaning rests with neither the one who creates nor the one who considers. Rather, it rests uneasily in the magic space between the two. Here, in the cool air of the cave, meanings might proliferate. Or they may scatter like dust and fade like pigment, especially if we hope for clean windows to a knowable past.

When viewing pictographs, most people, perhaps as a hedge against interpretive instability, first run through the representational possibilities. Look at that spider. That must be a bear, but its head is sort of human. And there's condor man. With Chumash rock art, however, it soon becomes clear that the most representational elements are stylized and account for only parts of the images. Moreover, much Chumash rock painting is not made to look like anything we've seen in the external world. Yet even the images that look like things we saw on the trail coming in might evoke associations that tell us more about ourselves than about those who created the images.

But this is the inescapable nature of interpretation. All interpretation involves an imaginative leap. Rare are the instances where we approach a work of art confident that we share the mindset and assumptions of the artist and the artist's community and culture. Yet we seem to forget this as we plunge into the experience of thinking we understand another even as we name our own desires and fears as the other's. The key to clearer, more comprehensive understanding may be to keep the imagination continually leaping rather than at rest. Perhaps interpretation can be likened to rock-hopping across Sespe Creek. Sometimes the chain of steps and jumps is clear from the bank; sometimes the path disappears midstream and backtracking is necessary. Occasionally, after some fruitless wandering along the bank, you make an ill-advised leap: You either make it across or get wet. Even standing dry on the far bank, you know more creek crossings are just around the bend in the trail. One man I've hiked with doesn't even look for a path of stones; he just wades right in, boots and all.

Wintu visual artist Frank LaPena, though speaking in general "Native American" terms and not about Chumash rock art specifically, suggests that rock art may continue to function as an art form of beauty that reveals "the world as it is" and a "traditional view of reality" (25). LaPena's comments apply well to Chumash art, even to the art in the cave above the creek. LaPena speaks of psychic abilities cultivated by traditional native peoples in ways that may make sense even to those skeptical of the transcendent. His ideas might also help us understand relationships between shamanistic practices and the natural environment. "For example," he writes, "a person who can project his/her mind to gain information from a distance is better understood, or easier to understand, if spoken of or drawn as a human-bird being" (25). LaPena attributes what he calls psychic abilities to a frame of reference grounded in a holistic worldview and the "principles of natural law," which I take to be the observable environment. In another context, Barry Lopez describes in *Of Wolves and Men* how the Nunamiut of Alaska develop powers of observation that seem amazing to outsiders, even trained wildlife biologists. For the Nunamiut, understanding wolves is an art. LaPena writes, "Art helps to create order; elements of this order are some concerns that continue to identify mankind's relationship to the bioethical responsibility of the way we choose to live, the way we relate our lives to the idea that there is a universal connection in all things" (25).

I find these ideas attractive, and that makes me wary. I'm a little uneasy attaching them to the term "shaman," though the scholarly consensus seems to be that shamans were mostly responsible for rock art in coastal Southern California. The problem is that the term has encouraged many vaguely supported cross-cultural generalizations. In addition to its use by New Age hucksters, "shaman" has been appropriated by many reputable scholars, writers, and visual artists to describe their own magic making. Since the term has been spread so thinly, I would love to avoid it altogether; however, it seems, given the evidence, to be a useful shorthand description for what some Chumash specialists were up to. Rick Bury, a photographer who has produced many fine images of Chumash rock art, raises an even more basic question that should give me pause: "Why would prehistoric art have been made only by sorcerers, when in every living culture nearly anyone can make art?" (152).

Interpretive rock-hopping aside, it may still be that the paintings in the cave give us a glimpse of how some people maintained their relationship to a place. But to approach that understanding, one must work backward through a good deal of turmoil and cultural disruption. It may be that the pictographs in this cave point not to undisturbed origins so much as to times of change and negotiation between cultures.

The life of Fernando Librado Kitsepawit, the Chumash gentleman who told the bear-man stories, gives us a sense of what it meant to live through these times. Fernando was born on Santa Cruz Island in 1804 and spent most of his life in and around the mainland town of Ventura. Born just following the major diphtheria epidemics of 1800–1802, Fernando would have been a young man at the time of the Chumash revolt in 1824. He lived through the secularization of the missions in 1834, was a vaquero for various ranches for many years, and spent the last two decades of his life—from age 90 to 111—as a handyman at the Las Cruces stage station west of Santa Barbara.

Some scholars suggest that since Fernando was born into a prominent family and had many contacts both on Santa Cruz Island and the mainland, he had great access to esoteric information that might otherwise have been closed off (Hudson, Blackburn, and Culetti 3). However, it is clear from his stories that while he obviously knew a great deal, some things were kept from him precisely because he occupied a position between cultures during a time of suspicion. The ethnographer J. P. Harrington reports that "If a person took toloache *Datura meteloides,* or jimsonweed, an alkaloid hallucinogen and he showed his faith, the old people would teach him all of those old things. But Fernando was familiar with the white people, and so they never taught him. The old ones were afraid that secrets about poisons and other mysteries would be given away, and they did not want to be punished or maybe even burned at the stake" (Hudson, Blackburn, and Culetti 42). As is common in colonial situations, negotiations between colonizer and colonized intensify in the areas of religion and ritual, the visible expressions of the most deeply held beliefs about the workings of the universe and people's place in it. Those who attempt to move between cultures and worldviews are often viewed with suspicion by both sides. Yet it is precisely their adeptness at border-crossing that frequently allows these mediators to survive. Fernando, who lived long during a time when survival was difficult, has the tension of his position between cultures put to him by an old Chumash man, who says to him:

As long as you live, Fernando, you will learn things from one
side—the Indian side—and from the other side—the Christian
side. But if you had lived with us, you would have learned
many things. Ah! It is too bad you have not lived with us. If

you had been brought up with us, you would have learned many Indian things. But you are by blood pure Chumash and know something, and will never leave this country. Remember Fernando, never to deny anything of either Indian or Christian sides and never to lie. These are two things to remember. When matters of jealousy and interest arise between Indians and Christians, they will fight and kill each other, but if you tell a lie, Fernando, they will kill you first. (Hudson, Blackburn, and Culetti 67–8)

The speech is marked by a curious combination of cultural dichotomy and confluence: never deny anything of either side. Yet the old man seems to have recognized in Fernando an inclination toward understanding traditional ways. It may be that under different circumstances Fernando's ability to move on the margins of two cultures would have found expression instead in the transformative role of the shaman. I wonder, too, whether the awareness that certain important insights had been kept from him made it easier for Fernando to talk to Harrington, who was writing down all the stories. After all, ignorance made it impossible to divulge what was meant to be private.

The most poignant scene from Fernando's life in the interstices of cultures comes when he asks one of the last of the bear dancers to teach him a Tulareño bear song (Hudson, Blackburn, and Culetti 81). After a time, the man gives up, saying that Fernando could not intone the song correctly, that his voice was better adapted to Spanish. Fernando recalls that he could not get the tremolo right, the way the old singers could. Though the bear song was never learned or translated for Harrington and the rest of us, the gaps in Fernando's stories reveal a great deal about the impulse to protect hard-earned knowledge from misuse. Or, perhaps we see a certain resignation on the part of those who were the last holders of knowledge that had accumulated for centuries. Knowledge, and moreover wisdom, is contextual, and when the context shifts, what good are the details?

As I try to imagine what Fernando may have felt in his role of translator between two cultures, I can't help but think of my own shifting contexts, trivial by comparison. Even sitting in the mouth of the cave, the paintings silent in the stony shadows behind me, I re-mind myself to put out the trash and recycling bins when I get home the next day. I wonder if I'll have time to change the oil in the truck that afternoon. And I know from experience that when I'm lying un-der the truck, wrench in hand, I'll dream of pictographs and flowing streams. My mind flits between city and wilderness even more often than my body. Perhaps to achieve internal coherence as much as any-thing, I feel the need to explain one side to the other. I want city people to know there is a place so nearby where beautiful creatures survive and where the past breaks through into our present. Walking the streets of LA, peering into the faces of so many sorts of people, I wonder whether the stories behind pictographs—or those of condors, sheep, and bears—could add meaning and grace to city lives.

So often, I find it difficult to explain even to my friends what the Sespe means to me and what it could mean to them, even if they never set foot in the backcountry. Partly, it's just that the quiet of a cave and the subtlety of its stories fade in the din of important projects at work, recent political developments, and the list of top-grossing films. When I describe time spent along the Sespe, I think people enmeshed in "real life" mostly hear of an escape; they hear of recreation rather than re-creation. I know from experience how easy it is to fall silent in the face of a culture that generally assumes the irrelevance of wilder-ness rivers and my way of seeing the world. In this I feel a dim kinship with those who came before me to this place, whose world suddenly seemed not to matter.

By the 1870s, when the last public ceremony of that time was per-formed, Chumash life had undergone profound transformations since 1542 when the Spanish explorer Juan Cabrillo sailed along the California coast. The impact on Chumash culture intensified when the Spanish built the missions in the 1770s and 1780s. Epidemics, the imposition of Catholicism, relocations, forced labor, sexual assaults, and natural environments altered by cattle, horses, and a new sort of agriculture were all part of a culture of crisis. During the epidemics between 1800 and 1802, for example, 15 percent of the Chumash at Mission Santa Barbara died (Castillo 47–61). Ironically, the high death rates at missions may have contributed to the survival of Chumash religious practices (Jackson and Castillo 36). As older recruits died, the Franciscans replaced them with unacculturated Indians who reintroduced traditional practices to others at the mission. The result was a mix of those who had turned toward the spiritual power of the Spanish priests because it seemed their own shamans were losing their effectiveness and those who turned toward ever more secretive and esoteric shamanistic practices.

After the failed revolt by the Chumash in 1824, ritual practice became even more reclusive. Scholars suggest that a combination of events led up to the revolt, including the appearance of a comet that foretold great changes and the approach of Easter confessions that disrupted ritual practices (Jackson and Castillo 78). The priests used the confessions to try to extract information in an effort to root out the ʔAntap movement, which maintained secretive ritual practices associated with toloache use and rock painting. Every major village contained a number of ʔAntap members, though members also traveled widely, linking villages throughout the Chumash area (Blackburn 13). According to Edward Castillo, ʔAntap traditions evolved into a messianic revitalization movement after missionization.

The revolt can therefore be seen as part of an effort to protect evolving forms of traditional religion. Following the revolt, many people fled the missions for the backcountry. It is possible that some rock art in the interior Coast and Transverse Ranges of Southern California may be the result of increased ritual activity that grew in response to the cultural stress of death by disease, overwork, lack of sanitation at the missions, and poor diet (Hudson and Underhay 72). It may be that the art in the cave I know arises not so much from a precontact Eden as a culture of crisis and exile.

The canyon I'm visiting would have been fairly hospitable to refugees from the coast and main river valleys. The creek would offer water in all but the driest years. The massive oak tree may have been small two hundred years ago, but other oaks, now dead, may have been bearing acorns, an essential staple. There is no doubt, however, that this place would have been considered remote from the larger surrounding villages. Lists of Chumash places, compiled mostly from mission records, include the nearest large villages whose names contemporary Southern Californians would recognize: "Piiru," "Matiliha," and "Sespe" (Heizer). There are also village sites in the Tehachapi Mountains to the north. All of these sites are many difficult trail miles from the cave. To be clear, my thoughts about the origins of the rock art are speculations. Sometimes we find ourselves enlightened by considering the merely possible, by testing even the unstable stones in the flow of stories.

Some suggest that to the Chumash during this time the universe was filled with power, and that the people lived at its geographical, psychological, and symbolic center (Hudson, Blackburn, and Culetti 5). Certain plants, animals, and places could be sources of power, and people could learn to acquire and manipulate it. Given the unpredictable and dangerous nature of the universe, it was necessary that humans do what they could to understand, and perhaps to predict and control, the flow of power. Indeed, the balance of power would be upset if people did nothing to meet their responsibility to maintain interdependencies (Bean 21–32). Shamans were the ones charged with such ritual maintenance, and it was they who acquired and used power to heal illness and disease. They did this by leaving the familiar surroundings of the community and moving toward the unknown physically as well as psychically. The safety and security of home and the village was in a tense balance with the unpredictability of the sacred and the space away from the village. It was the shaman who mediated between the two. Yet since power could be used for either good or ill, shamans were viewed ambivalently by their communities. They were seen as eccentric, though they held high social positions.

If shamans came to this cave, whether in times of cultural stress or prior to that, its remoteness and uniqueness would have served their needs well. Caves and unusual rock formations, as well as permanent water sources such as lakes, streams, and springs, were understood to be portals to the sacred realm where the power distributed across the landscape might be more accessible. Rock art might represent shamans' visions at these sites and may have functioned to help the shaman remember the visions and renew his power (Whitley 10).

Although we cannot know for sure how things looked from their perspective, the painters of these images may have given us a narrow glimpse of how they understood the interconnectedness of their world. We should understand, first of all, that by ingesting hallucinogens and entering a trance, a shaman was not seeking to leave "this world." As David Abram points out in his lyrical account of shamanistic ties to landscapes, westerners commonly assume that the "supernatural" must somehow be entirely separate from a deterministic and mechanical natural world (8). This accustomed view of the world may make it difficult to understand that the shaman alters his perception to contact the animistic forces that appear otherwise as mere scenery. This, Abram says, defines a shaman:

> the ability to readily slip out of perceptual boundaries that de-
> marcate his or her particular culture—boundaries reinforced
> by social customs, taboos, and most importantly, the common
> speech or language—in order to make contact with, and learn
> from, the other powers in the land. His magic is precisely this
> heightened receptivity to the meaningful solicitations—songs,
> cries, gestures—of the larger, more-than-human field. (9)

Imagine the forms in the cave that seem both human and animal. There is a figure with the wings of a condor and a humanlike head. One figure that may be a bear or a man, or both, is drawn in black and outlined with both white and red pigment. The Chumash believed in transmorphism, the ability of humans to take on the form of bears, or of other animals to occasionally take human form (Blackburn 40). Such transformations were not remarkable, since animals and plants were transformations of the First People and no inherent separation existed between humans and nonhumans (Blackburn 41). The possibility of transformation encouraged a sense of equality and interconnectedness. The shamans were not so much constructing a view of the world as representing a reality that we now articulate through ecological science, with its understanding of the interdependence of all parts of an ecosystem, which we often think of using the metaphor of a web.

For the Chumash, such visual representations could maintain their presence as part of the natural world. They seem to have lived surrounded by metaphors that made the world no less real, as when Harrington reports that his informant, María Solares, "has seen rocks in the mountains that are the exact shape of human arms and hands: they are the remains of people who died in the flood" (Blackburn 95). I've seen rocks like these in the Sespe, too, enough to remind me of the biblical prophet Ezekiel's valley of dry bones. Other pictographic figures may represent qualities of the transformative experience, yet as metaphors they take cues from observable reality. Amphibious animals such as frogs and salamanders, and lizards, which pass easily between rocks, were seen as messengers between the mundane and supernatural worlds and as metaphors for the shaman's ability to move between those worlds (Whitley 20). On my walks through the Sespe, I experience such metaphors continually. Ubiquitous alligator lizards scoot down the trail just ahead of my boots until they dart away to disappear under rocks. At creek crossings, I might see the now-endangered red-legged frog leap from the bank to glide from view beneath the water.

Perhaps the most remarkable painting in the cave I am visiting has the body and feet of a salamander with the fantail of a crayfish or lobster. The black, torpedo-shaped body is outlined in red, and its bulbous, three-toed feet grip the wall while a line moves from its head to a disk with rays. "Antennae" extend from this sunlike disk. In the 1960s, Campbell Grant made paintings of these pictographs showing white dots on the black bodies of this figure and the bear figure mentioned above. Nearly forty years later, I can't see the dots on the salamander, and those on the bear I take to be random disturbances of the pigment. One might ponder the irony that these creatures—frogs and salamanders especially—once the source of transformational metaphors, seem most sensitive to climate and habitat changes. Like their images in pigment, they are fading.

The salamander figure recalls a Chumash metaphor for a trancelike state, that of going under water or drowning (Whitley 23). If you imagine the weightlessness of swimming, with the refraction of light that skews sight and the muffled sounds, it's not hard to understand the physical logic of this metaphor for entering a trance (Whitley 23). Other metaphors for trance included sexual intercourse and its associations with womblike caves, and the phrase "entering the canoe," which is represented at a rock art site in San Luis Obispo County (Whitley 167). It's not hard to understand their physical logic, either. Each of these visionary metaphors evidences a view of the world formed through careful observation. The creatures put to use as metaphor serve in ways fitting to their natures. The metaphors conserve their typical behaviors and ways of being in the world, and each mode of being has to do with transformation. They testify to a world that flexes forever according to certain rules and tendencies.

If we consider rock art as part of the transformative process of shamans, we begin to contemplate notions that might seem paradoxical. Although the shaman's transformation was a way to leave the temporal and physical world, its representation is unmistakably here and now, marked on stone. Although the shaman left this world to seek the power of the cosmos, it was to understand more completely the world that is with us. Shamans sought a measure of control in an uncertain world without the illusion of complete control. And although shamans had cultivated their ways of tapping the world's power over precontact centuries, they tried to the end to put their knowledge to use in a period of cultural transformation.

Because the shaman relinquishes his own perspective for that of others, he ties the parts of the world together. Or, more precisely, the shaman is privileged with a glimpse of the world's completeness. Twentieth-century minds may wish to relegate this process to a romanticized mysticism. But we should remember that such transformations are also made possible, along with the resulting good or evil for the community, within the context of careful, passed-along knowledge of botany, meteorology, zoology, psychology, and other divisions of what we now call science. In fact, the Chumash shaman's view of the universe meshes with the more recent ideas of ecologists who no longer see balance and stability so much as constant fluctuation and disturbance where random events have unpredictable effects. The world was not a wilderness Eden of perfect harmony but a dangerous place of constant change in which people intervened for their own benefit and protection. They realized, however, that the most successful interventions would be backed by an awareness of interrelationships and a knowledge that good for people aligned with good for all parts of the environment.

If people assume that many parts of the natural environment have the same qualities of sentience, will, rationality, and emotion that humans possess, then plants, animals, birds—perhaps even some special rocks—are part of the social world to which people belong (Blackburn 66). Such a view of the world may result in a sense of environmental responsibility that Western science and legal systems are only beginning to articulate and encourage. The Chumash seemed to see humans as primarily responsible for maintaining the interdependency of all the world's parts. Perhaps they understood that such responsibility came with the power to manipulate and disrupt. Since the world was in continual flux, it required continual ritual and practical attention. Shamans would not have been surprised that power shifted with the coming of the Spanish, but they may have been taken aback by the scope and speed of cultural and environmental change. They may have felt desperate just to stay in the game.

I imagine ʔAntap shamans in a cave deep in the wilderness painting their visions, trying to right the world with what little power remained. They remembered a world that mostly made sense, even if it was at times unpredictable, and they spoke in a language that could articulate these memories. Looking at their images, feeling comparatively little, it's not hard to believe that the world's power has diminished or withdrawn from us, we who seldom even acknowledge our relationships to the creatures and places we are bound to despite our ignorance.

It may be appropriate that these pictographs often leave me with a vague aesthetic response as I try to envision—through the pigment, the stone, and the surroundings—a time when things mostly fit together and people could be counted on to try to maintain this fittingness. But what if we could understand the act of interpreting pictographs as an attempt at transformation—the leaving of our own perspectives for those of others? In looking at the paintings and thinking about them, I'm not sure how much of myself I've managed to leave behind. Yet I think I've seen something new. Perhaps all that's left is the merest glimpse revealing the interdependency of all things. Perhaps this is something for which to be thankful.

CHAPTER 5

The River Flows

Dam Ideas and Double Crosses

But that same image, we ourselves see in all rivers and oceans.
It is the image of the ungraspable phantom of life; and this is
the key to it all. —HERMAN MELVILLE, *Moby Dick*

Some years after the walls of a cave were painted, at about the time the last of the Sespe's grizzlies were dying or being killed, people relatively new to the area began to think of ways to kill off the wildness of the stream itself. They wanted to put the water to good use. To the east and west of Sespe Creek run two streams whose fates highlight the Sespe's uniqueness. If you drive along Interstate 5 between Bakersfield and Los Angeles, you'll notice part of one of them. You won't recognize it as Piru (say Pie'roo) Creek, though. You'll see the creek dammed to create, along with water from the eastern Sierra Nevada, Pyramid Lake, crosshatched on a warm Saturday by Jet Skis jumping one another's wakes. Boats circle, pulling wake-boarders and skiers. Piru Creek runs east from high in a proposed addition to the Sespe Wilderness and bends toward the south to where it has been dammed to produce what all dams advertise—drinking water, flood control, electricity, and recreation. The creek reappears below the dam to wind for fifteen miles before it meets Lake Piru just below its confluence with Agua Blanca Creek, which also flows from the Sespe backcountry. In dry years, when the level of the lake has dropped, Piru Creek cuts a path through the sediment it has deposited in the reservoir.

Sediment has almost entirely filled in the dam on Matilija Creek to the west of the Sespe, rendering it useless for flood control, water reclamation, or recreation. It is simply a cement wall with a shallow lake and a mudflat thicket where the reservoir used to be. But just because the dam is useless does not mean it is harmless. The Matilija, like Sespe Creek, Piru Creek, and many other streams tying the upper elevations to the ocean, is a historical steelhead run. The dam stands between the oceangoing steelhead trout and its prime spawning habitat. In recent years the Matilija Dam has become a poster child in dam-removal efforts. Bruce Babbitt, while he was secretary of the interior under Bill Clinton, even stood atop the dam with his symbolic sledgehammer. Actual removal, however, won't begin until a study-in-progress figures out the best way to remove the tons of sediment that has collected over decades.

The Sespe, bracketed by these two dammed streams, runs freely. The one thing that could have irrevocably changed the essence of Sespe Creek and its surroundings never happened. Why? Why did the Sespe survive when the waters of so many other rivers and streams were controlled, collected, and put to human use? How did the Sespe survive an ethic that considered in-stream flows wasteful, almost sinful? How did the Sespe flow into a time when its wildness could be valued for reasons other than possession and profit? When I look at the Sespe's present rugged remoteness, I'm tempted to say the Sespe saved the Sespe—a charismatic landscape active in its own defense. But that's not fair to Matilija Creek or Piru Creek. The Sespe's present freedom has more to do with the worst and best of what humans have to offer. The story begins in gunfights, double crosses, and shady schemes. It ends with environmental activism and an act of Congress.

After spending the morning carving turns and spinning my kayak in blissful winter surf at Ventura, I stop at the John Nichols Gallery in Santa Paula to look at a collection of historical snapshots of the Sespe region. After I greet his big orange cat, Sespe Red, Nichols leads me through paintings and photographs by local artists and up the stairs to the loft of the old hardware store. After arranging a light over a desk, he leaves me perusing several albums and some old documents. One title catches my eye: "Sespe Light and Power Company." I glance between the company's articles of incorporation, dated 1915, and the photographs meant to prove to potential shareholders that Sespe Creek carried enough water to make a series of dams profitable.

One snapshot shows three well-dressed men, presumably the company's representatives, standing beside a car on a dirt road carved into the slope above Sespe Creek. The car carries two spare tires riding the front fenders behind the bug-eye headlights. The road, I presume, runs from Fillmore up the Sespe toward Devil's Gate, a narrow gap in the canyon. It is likely one of the Sespe roads destined to decline to a trail, before lack of maintenance, washouts, and aggressive chaparral make even the trail difficult to follow. The men in the photo stand a little uneasily on the gravel in their leather dress shoes. Their suits, ties, and overcoats fit well. They look like they would be more comfortable in downtown Los Angeles on level concrete near their offices. One man looks down out of the frame toward the creek. I wonder what he sees. Does he intuit that the creek anchors an ecosystem, even though he would not have used such language? Does he see a stream that can change its landscape overnight in a flood or wait patiently in deep pools during dry years? Or does he see pavement, profit, and permanence? Progress.

The company named for my favorite stream no longer exists, but it had grand goals for a short time. Sespe Light and Power was created in 1915 to raise money from shareholders. It's possible that raising money was the founders' chief intention and that actually doing anything other than enriching themselves was secondary. Nevertheless, the idea was there to dam the Sespe in five places to hold winter storms and spring runoff and generate electricity. This was the first comprehensive proposal to put the stream to use, and dams were only the beginning. The articles of incorporation leave no stone unturned and no water unaccounted for in stating the company's purpose "to locate, claim, divert, and otherwise acquire water and water rights under the laws of the State of California for all purposes; to construct, acquire and maintain ditches, dams, tunnels, levees, viaducts, bridges, embankments and excavations, to, across and from any water course, lake, stream, or water way" (Sespe Light and Power Company). The Sespe was to become one way of interpreting what it means to have dominion over the earth.

The story of the massive effort to control water in California is, of course, one of hubris. We are still coming to terms with the ecological consequences of a century of dam building. For flood control, drinking water, power, and irrigation, rivers were blocked in over fourteen hundred places throughout the state. The biggest projects piped water from the eastern Sierra Nevada to Los Angeles and captured snowmelt in reservoirs along the western slope of the Sierra. Today, many roads leading into the mountains wind around "lakes" whose bathtub rings gauge the previous winter's snowpack. During the era of dam and aqueduct building—that is, the second half of the nineteenth century and most of the twentieth—some desert valleys became fertile farmland while other fertile valleys were returned to the deserts. Salmon and steelhead runs first smothered by silt from hydraulic mining during the gold rush were now blocked altogether by dams without fish ladders. Gradually, such available water addicted California to seemingly limitless growth of both population and crops, though periodically we discover that the rivers don't stretch far enough. One winter of "subnormal" snowpack precipitates battles the following summer between farmers who claim rights to "their" irrigation water and the defenders of the water rights of endangered fish species. But even where there seems to be plenty of water, problems crop up. In some parts of the San Joaquin Valley—America's true breadbasket—irrigation has salinated soils to the point where they will no longer grow crops. Though the need for a paradigm shift in water use may seem obvious to some, U.S. president George W. Bush talks of diverting the rivers of British Columbia south.

Compared to the biggest California water projects, the Sespe was a drop in the bucket, but it was nevertheless seen as flowing water that should not be wasted. Its seasonal volume was enough to suggest profit and to draw investors who could purchase shares in the dream of controlling nature. The capital stock of the Sespe Light and Power Company was to be a million dollars divided into one million shares. Shareholders could see themselves as part of a larger narrative of progress. As with so many resource extraction schemes, notions of the public good masked the greed of a few.

In 1915, the men of Sespe Light and Power had reason to be optimistic. Two years earlier, William Mulholland, who designed an irrigation system for Sespe water in 1887, had completed the famous aqueduct bringing water to Los Angeles from the Owens Valley east of the Sierra Nevada. "There it is. Take it," said Mulholland as the water tumbled down the spillway into the San Fernando Valley, which was annexed by Los Angeles to the enrichment of land speculators. Also in 1913, Congress approved, in spite of the opposition of John Muir and the Sierra Club, the damming of the Tuolumne River to fill Hetch Hetchy Valley and provide water for San Francisco.

Perhaps it was the Sespe's relative insignificance that allowed it to survive the hydrological gold rush. Unlike the larger projects, it did not attract the best minds or most powerful pockets. Ironically, it may be that the Sespe survives as the only major free-flowing stream in Southern California partly because of overreaching greed and ambition.

Indeed, avarice and bullying were the foundations of the Sespe Light and Power Company. Its articles of incorporation may have lent an aura of seriousness to its pursuits and its threat to the Sespe, but the tone of its history descends toward tragicomedy. Of its board of directors, only one man, by the name of Mason Bradfield, leaves a historical trace. It appears that the company may have been a sham by which Bradfield hoped to profit from public investment. The boyish-faced Bradfield had earlier in life been the protégé of Joe Dye, a notoriously ill-tempered gunslinger whose thuggery was excused by his position as a lawman. After Bradfield defied Dye by filing a claim in the Sespe under his own name rather than Dye's, the two had a falling out, and Bradfield ambushed Dye, killing him with a shotgun on a street in Los Angeles. Bradfield was acquitted, despite his obvious guilt, by a jury quite familiar with Dye's bullying.

Bradfield's inclination to dealing violently with rivals showed itself again in securing the rights of Sespe Light and Power. While the company claimed rights to water, oil, brownstone, and recreational opportunities in the upper Sespe, its access to these lands was blocked by one man, George Henley, who owned property at Devil's Gate, where the river passes through a narrow sandstone gap above Fillmore. Henley had set up camp at the Gate and instituted a toll on hunters and fishermen who wished to pass into the backcountry. Once Bradfield's company had built a road up to Henley's camp, Henley is said to have charged five dollars for Cadillacs and fifty cents for Model T Fords. Henley's fees generated considerable ill will among the sportsmen, who considered it their right to use the Sespe.

When the conflict between the two men reached a head during a dispute over a survey, Bradfield shot Henley in the back. Henley survived, and Bradfield was charged with assault with a deadly weapon. Though convicted, Bradfield received a light sentence after the mayor of Los Angeles and other prominent businessmen took the witness stand to testify to his character. Los Angeles attorneys produced certificates concerning his ill health, and though the illness was not named, there were suggestions of insanity.

When Bradfield was released from prison, he began to revive Sespe Light and Power. The company's last gasp took the form of an engineering report in 1921 that detailed the viability of the business plan. The report emphasized the company's potential diversification beyond water and power to oil, sandstone, and the recreation that the reservoirs would encourage. As in the photographs, the magical qualities of the Sespe seep through the evidence of its fitness as a resource: "the Sespe has cut a very deep gash into the territory, cutting through the heavy beds of altered shales and sandstones, that pitch with the direction of flow. This condition of erosion is responsible for the numerous wide spaces for reservoir sites, each followed by a narrow cut through a resistant dyke, forming excellent dam sites" (Eastwood).

As I read this description, it occurs to me that these same geological processes are responsible for the rhythms of travel I've become accustomed to in the Sespe. I regularly experience the constriction in the narrow cuts that gives way to the release of grassy meadows and wide views in the flats where the reservoirs would be. The Sespe is the natural equivalent of an old European city, with its shadowy slot-canyon streets leading to lightened plazas. Neither the Sespe nor the city would compel such subtle shades of emotion without the tension of the contrast.

Other Sespe Light and Power photos show the abundance of the Sespe's water—deep pools, cascading side creeks, river-wide ledge holes. Quarryable sandstone inclines toward the stream. The black-and-white images could be typical snapshots by a present-day hiker trying to capture the beauty of the place. The scenes are unpeopled and serene. As I look at them I feel the excited anticipation I associate with spring wildflower season when I hear the creek before I open my eyes in the morning. In my mind I wait through the chill for the sun, knowing by noon I'll stop walking to take a dip in a blue-green eddy. As I shuffle through the old snapshots, I imagine the cascading trill of canyon wrens.

I wonder about the photographer. The photos show grains of aesthetic sensitivity that contrast with their utilitarian purpose. There is some attention to composition. They don't just document water; they suggest its compelling, continuous, attractive flowing. What did he (I presume) feel while he spent time in the backcountry? Was he simply doing his work, or did the place work on him?

I flip to the next photo to see a truck passing a mule-drawn wagon on the road above the stream. I think of the canyon as a place of work, where men put their weight into the swing of a pickaxe or set blasting caps to clear boulders from where the road is to be. I imagine a man working along the Sespe for weeks at a time might come to appreciate its presence and value it for more than the wealth it might yield. It would depend, I suppose, mostly on the man. I flip back a few photos to the well-dressed men by the fancy automobile. It looks to me like they are glad to be on merely a day trip from LA. They are the ones with ideas, whose money puts the other men to work and the beauty to good use. But this would not be true for long. The money ran out, the work stopped, and the company went bust.

But for the tragicomic demise of Sespe Light and Power, these photos might have become a minor entry into the genre of memorials to rivers that were. I'm thinking of David Brower's stunning films and Katie Lee's still shots of Glen Canyon on the Colorado, and of John Pfahl's photographs of reservoirs beneath which rest inundated rock art sites and ancient structures. I'm thinking of Edward Abbey's essays on the Dolores River and Glen Canyon. When I hike through an area along the Sespe once intended for inundation, I sometimes imagine myself beneath acre-feet of water. I picture the silt accumulating where I stand and motorboats pulling water-skiers around and around above my head.

The Sespe Light and Power Company project was merely the first of many attempts to harness the Sespe's flow that never got beyond the planning stages. In 1925, the Ojai Irrigation District proposed a dam at Cold Springs, high in the mountains north of the town. In 1932 the Santa Clara Water Conservation District drew up a map of the Cold Springs site. A 1949 map from the Ventura County Flood Control District has reservoirs penciled in at Devil's Gate and Cold Springs, as well as one in the middle beneath the Topatopa bluffs in the Sespe Condor Sanctuary. In 1957, the U.S. Bureau of Reclamation proposed dams at Topatopa and Tar Creek as well as a conduit through a mountain to take water to a valley north of the city of Thousand Oaks. However, the United (formerly Santa Clara) Water Conservation District claimed prior water rights and stopped the bureau.

Ideas for two of the old dam sites were resurrected in 1967 in what would turn out to be a very close call for the Sespe. The United Water Conservation District proposed a $90 million bond issue to create dams at Topatopa and further upstream at Cold Springs. A pipeline would carry the water to the village of Saticoy in the Santa Clara Valley between Santa Paula and Ventura. Letters to the local newspaper touted the statistics meant to curry public favor: a $55 million payroll, 4,800 man-years of employment, and approximately $39 million in federal funds for recreation and sport-fishing facilities. It was estimated that recreation alone would create an industry of $12 million annually. The project, it was claimed, would also save $550,000 per year in flood damages, along with "incalculable savings in human life and misery." The Ventura County Economic Development Association, the County Farm Bureau, the Building and Construction Trades Council, and the cities of Port Hueneme, Santa Paula, and Fillmore all supported the issue.

Simultaneously, hydrologists cited the need to relieve the overuse of groundwater that was allowing seawater to move inland to contaminate wells in the Santa Clara Valley. Interestingly, the replenishment of aquifers is presently cited as one of the primary benefits of the Vern Freeman Diversion Dam on the Santa Clara River. The Freeman Diversion remains as the most significant obstacle preventing southern steelhead trout from reaching their spawning grounds in the Sespe. The boosters of the United Water proposal in 1967, however, claimed that the projects were necessary for wildlife protection and would somehow even "create" twenty-four miles of year-round trout stream. Since the reservoirs would have obviously inundated large sections of the Sespe, the newly "created" trout stream presumably would owe its existence to new roads allowing anglers to fish portions of the Sespe previously reached only by difficult miles on horseback or foot. If you couldn't drive to it, it didn't count. On the other side of the issue, researchers in the Sespe Condor Sanctuary, which had been established in 1947, claimed that reservoirs and increased recreational traffic so near crucial nesting sites would irreparably harm the condor's progress toward recovery.

The reason for all the campaigning was that the bond issue required a public vote. Though boosters created the appearance of widespread support, the measure failed by thirty-nine votes in a small, countywide election. Yet despite the narrow defeat of an ambitious project, the Sespe still had no permanent protection.

Protection came after much wrangling in the late 1980s and early 1990s. The process began when U.S. Congressman Robert Lagomarsino from Ventura introduced a bill to protect from development and dam building twenty-seven and a half of the most remote miles of the stream. Lagomarsino's bill was based on a U.S. Forest Service recommendation in a new management plan for the Los Padres. As with most environmental protection legislation, this proposal was criticized from both sides. Some said the bill didn't protect enough of the

Sespe; some said it protected too much. Environmentalists, including the fledgling organization Keep the Sespe Wild, called for protecting the whole of the Sespe. They argued that the bill specifically left open the possibility for two dams in well-known sites on the upper and lower portions of the river. Reservoirs in these sites would submerge unique geological formations and Chumash rock art sites and trap the sediment that replenishes ocean beaches and protects beachfront homes from sea erosion. They also pointed out that the Oat Mountain dam site just above Fillmore rested directly over the San Cayetano fault, capable of producing a seven-point earthquake.

On the other side of the issue, those who hoped to benefit from harnessing the Sespe tried to claim the public's best interest, just as their forebears had decades earlier. Water consultants and development proponents argued that any protection for the Sespe would rob Ventura County of valuable water for crops and population growth. They worried that Lagomarsino's bill would foreclose the Topatopa dam site, which could provide the greatest storage capacity. On this last point, the congressman appeared to compromise in favor of the environment, though he must have known a reservoir in the heart of the condor sanctuary would never be politically feasible. Opponents of the bill also characterized the Sespe as dangerously unpredictable and argued that dams were needed to prevent a recurrence of the 1969 flood that killed a number of people and caused millions of dollars of damage downstream along the Santa Clara River. The debate over the bill received national attention in 1991 when the nationwide river conservation organization American Rivers included the Sespe in its annual list of the most threatened waterways.

Eventually, after amendments and debate, the Los Padres Condor Range and River Protection Act became law in 1992. The statistics are stunning: 400,450 acres of newly designated wilderness, including the 219,700-acre Sespe Wilderness. Thirty-one and a half miles of Sespe Creek received wild and scenic status, and an additional ten miles was declared a wild and scenic study river. The four miles added to the twenty-seven and a half of the original bill came about when river conservation groups successfully challenged the Forest Service's management plan as arbitrary. By the time the bill passed, even water boosters began to suggest that the decades of debate about the Sespe had distracted Ventura County from developing other, more economically viable water sources. It had become clear that the cost of building a dam would raise the price of water beyond what farmers and residents could afford. Furthermore, other water districts in Southern California were proving that more water could be made available through conservation than could ever be collected from a seasonal creek like the Sespe.

A great deal of credit for preserving the Sespe goes to the analysis and arguments that activists used to sway legislators and the public. Yet a less tangible force was at work as well—the powerful pull of a beautiful place. While aesthetic and spiritual values often seem insubstantial, even slightly awkward, up against the facts and figures of resource development, they nevertheless carry weight, and those working to save the Sespe knew this. They knew they could move legislators only if the place itself moved their constituents. And it did. Activists produced videos of hikers enjoying the Sespe's grand vistas and fly fishers casting in clear pools. Local photographers and painters put up exhibitions that transformed scenery into art. Unlike with the photographs composed to support fund-raising for the first Sespe dam project in the first decades of the twentieth century, the beauty of the Sespe in recent photography and painting is not an accidental by-product. It is good in itself. Through art, people who would never visit the remote Sespe came to value its presence. Wallace Stegner suggested that wilderness benefits even those who only drive up to its edge and look in. In fact, the integrity and reassurance of wild places may be communicated at still greater distances.

Framed by Matilija Creek and Piru Creek, the Sespe exists as if in parentheses, a remark separated from the general narrative but speaking the truth almost as an afterthought. Water, left to its own devices, lives and breathes. From capillary rivulets and heart-water springs, it gathers a whole landscape to itself. Its character finds expression as rainfall and snowmelt following a path of their own making. Autumn pools reflect the sky, then blink to reveal the depths. Shifting and shaping its landscape, a stream flexes and stretches over time. The forms a creek takes on its own will prove more surprising, subtle, and inspiring than those we might build to constrain it. We might forget this if not for the Sespe swirling past sandstone the color of blood and skin.

CHAPTER 6

Crude Visions

Oil in the Sespe

> *It gathers to a greatness, like the ooze of oil*
> *Crushed.*
>
> —GERARD MANLEY HOPKINS, "God's Grandeur"

Sespe Creek itself narrowly avoided condemnation, but the banks of its lower reaches and the hillsides above its deepest gorge bear the drilling pads, access roads, and pipelines of profitable enterprise. How to think of these marks in the middle of the wilderness isn't at all clear to me. The essence of the Sespe has clearly survived, but I still wonder what it would be like without the intrusion.

These are my thoughts as I steer my truck up exceedingly steep, narrow roads into the Sespe Oil Field. It feels good to ignore the KEEP OUT! warnings at the entrance and enter new territory instead of driving past on the way to a trailhead, as I have many times. I always look for good reasons to pass a NO TRESPASSING sign. As the song says, "on the other side, it didn't say nothin' / This land was made for you and me." I'm here to meet a man who has observed this part of the Sespe longer than almost anyone. Since 1963, Jim Day has spent most of his working days high in the mountains above Sespe Creek in one of California's oldest oil fields. He works as a "pumper," or lease operator, keeping the wells in working order, looking for potential problems, checking gauges, and recording flows. Day and two others are eating lunch when I arrive at the shack. One of the first things he says to me: "Some days are beautiful up here; some days it's the most miserable place on earth."

I know a bit of what he means. At many levels—weather, ecology, history—the greater Sespe is a place of surprising contrasts, not least of which is its geographical embrace of an oil field. It's something you can ignore for only so long. I've avoided it for a while, perhaps because it conjures up uncomfortable tensions in me and in this place I'm growing rather attached to. My life begins with water, not oil. The two don't mix. Water is clear, creative, and quick. Oil is dark, toxic, and slow until burned. Water is birth; oil is death. Water flows through our bodies; oil should not. I depend on water . . . and yet I depend almost as much on oil.

Beautiful and miserable. Today is closer to the former, even in the oil field. When the air is still, the mid-February sun feels like spring, but I reach for a jacket when the brisk breeze kicks up. Stinging lupine, mountain lilac, and fiesta flower bloom on the south slopes. Clouds are beginning to collect around the tops of the mountains, and it will probably rain tonight. While Day finishes some paperwork in the shack, I stand outside looking across a maze of dirt roads and oil pads. In the foreground, pipelines plunge through the brush, sometimes spanning washes like suspension bridges where the soil has eroded beneath them. Here and there, piles of rusty old pipes and used-up parts sit abandoned. When the wind shifts, I can hear the drone of fans from the natural gas compressors a half mile away across a valley.

The oil field is nearly surrounded by the Sespe Condor Sanctuary and the Hopper Mountain National Wildlife Refuge. On a map, the oil field appears to be an intrusion into the official protected areas it predates. If you look at maps of the western United States, you will find many such arrangements. Wilderness boundaries were drawn to exclude the less than pristine and to allow the resource extraction to continue. On maps, the narrow paths and the strip mines and oil fields they lead to sometimes look like lollipops or mushroom clouds. The Sespe Oil Field's "intrusion" is not so extreme—more like a shark fin or a mountain against the sky. But on the ground, the lines between wilderness and not-wilderness aren't so clear. From an oil access road I visually trace deer trails across windblown, tall-grass meadows. Flocks of tiny birds—maybe bushtits—flow in waves through the brush, and a red-tailed hawk flashes overhead in full stoop. A northern harrier patrols the next ridge over. Oil pads and raptors, this place is stunningly beautiful. The human imprint on the landscape is unmistakable, but the wildness radiates nevertheless. This is evident even in a description of the oil field in an old annual report issued by the California Division of Oil and Gas: "The topography is extremely rugged; elevations range between 600 and 4,200 feet, with an average well elevation of 2,200 feet. The area is drained by a series of perennial and intermittent streams that flow westward into Sespe Creek which in turn flows south to the Santa Clara River" (Dosch 39). In the 1967 report, paragraphs listing various oil field sectors and well operators ("The productive area consists of 1,200 acres in Secs. 4, 5 and 6, T.4 N., R.19 W . . .") bracket descriptions of persistent wildness: "Much of the terrain is covered with a dense, almost impregnable chaparral, although oaks abound in certain areas, and on the higher ridges yellow pines are dispersed with the chaparral. The area, which includes part of the Sespe Wildlife Domain, has an annual rainfall of 30 to 50 inches" (39). The effect of the juxtaposition reflects my experience of the tensions in this beautiful, working landscape.

Day joins me outside and lights a cigarette. "There's about all the wildlife you could want up here," he says. "I've had bears stand with their paws on the window sill, looking at me in the shack. We see bobcats almost every day."

When Day finishes his smoke, we get in his truck and head up to adjust a drilling unit that sits on a pad at about 3,500 feet above sea level. Another pumper, who works a different section of the field, takes his own truck to help out. At the well, the giant steel horse head is motionless. Earlier, Day had shut down the well after he noticed it was hitting bottom over 3,000 feet below in the Basal Sespe formation. From the bed of the truck, the two lean on and lift a wrench sizable enough to use for bench presses. They raise the depth of the drill string's plunge by about a hand's width. After retightening the adjustment mechanism, Day starts the unit and the horse head begins to bob. He lets the oily rod slide lightly through his fingers to check for vibration. There is none, and it seems the adjustment has done the trick. The two stand watching and listening for a few minutes to make sure nothing slips. Just up the road a quarter mile or so stands what's left of the cabin Carl Koford used while conducting research on condors beginning in 1939. The OPEN HOUSE sign out front is still there, and the shack is indeed open—to wind, birds, and whatever else might happen along.

Finally, the other man slams the tailgate of his truck and drives off to check leases in the Tar Creek area. Day and I walk over to where he resets the timer that turns the drilling unit on and off. Since the pump can pull more oil than the subterranean pool can produce, it shuts down periodically to wait for the pool to replenish.

As Day is explaining this to me, the truck roars back onto the pad. We walk over to see what's up, but Day stops abruptly about ten feet from the driver-side door. With one hand on the wheel, the driver tries to hold and hide a four-foot gopher snake in the other. He grasps it behind its head while its body wraps around his forearm. The snake is pale from spending the winter underground. "They're out early," he grins. "And if the gopher snakes are out, so are the rattlers." Day hates snakes, and he's not too excited by the news. "Rattlers are always hanging around in the equipment," he says. "They like the shade or cool metal in the summer. Time to keep an eye out." We watch as the snake slowly makes its way across the gravel toward the brush at the edge of oil pad. It crosses to safety without being snatched by one of the many raptors cruising the area. I walk to the edge of the oil pad and look far down into the Sespe over the Tar Creek drainage. To the northwest, the West Fork Sespe slides between Topatopa Peak and Bear Heaven.

In the Sespe, you can't fail to pay attention to where you are and what's happening around you. The surfaces shimmer with life and light even in the oil field. The men who work here know this, and they pay attention. But to them, the subsurface is also real, whereas my experience with the geology of the Sespe is mostly one of surface-level appreciation. Many of the trails into the backcountry begin in higher elevations and descend through geologic strata to Sespe Creek, which, along with its tributaries, carves a path through the uplifted layers of sediment and stone. As I've walked these trails, I've often contemplated the hues and textures of different varieties of sandstone. Sometimes I'll stand on a midstream gravel bar and try to trace the path of mauve and ocher chips to their sources in the surrounding hills. Sometimes, stones at the edge of the stream bear the curlicue imprints of shells. Once, I stepped over a midtrail log to find four fossil oyster shells arranged symmetrically by a previous passerby who must have wanted followers to notice and appreciate them. I left them where they were for the next person to happen upon.

Oil pulls my awareness deeper, so to speak, and the official state oil reports are a good start. To me, they represent a symbolic approach to looking at a landscape where surface details hint at hidden foundations.

Take, for example, the oil well named "Mel Blanc" for its former owner, who gave voice to classic Warner Brothers cartoon characters. Day and I drove by this well on the way up to adjust the other, and the 1967 annual report includes a cross-section diagram of its subsurface journey. Mel Blanc sits on a pad at 2,533 feet above sea level. From the surface, its drill string descends through just over 400 feet of the Rincon layer before passing through the thin, 200-foot Vaqueros stratum. From there, it continues through the Upper, Middle, and Basal Sespe formations.

A few miles from Mel Blanc, you can experience the surface manifestations of the oil well's descent by walking the trail that follows Tar Creek down to Sespe Creek. The trail begins at an elevation of 2,503 feet at the edge of the Rincon formation, which the 1967 report describes as of Lower Miocene age. It is composed of "mostly mudstone, while the lower part is predominantly shale with numerous thin beds containing dolomitic and limonitic concretions ranging up to two feet in diameter. The formation was deposited in a marine, shallow-

water environment" (Dosch 44). As you walk along the old road between walls of greasewood, you might notice the Rincon's bluish-
black, gray-brown, spheroidally fracturing shale poking up through
the brush on a nearby hillside. Soon, though, the shale gives way to
the dark gray or buff sandstone and siltstone of the Vaqueros formation, also of Miocene origin. The Vaqueros is composed of "thin
interbeds of sandy limestone containing numerous oyster shells" (45).

Crossing Tar Creek about a mile down the trail, the road becomes
a rough trail. You may stop to notice the rainbow of sandstone
pebbles at the stream's edge carried down from the sedimentary layers
above. As the trail resumes on the other side, you follow the contours
of the hills, crossing small streams flush with silt. Here and there
blood sandstone boulders crop up above the chaparral. Slowly, you
descend through the Oligocene Sespe formation, a varied layer composed of medium-grade sandstone and conglomerate, with shale inter-
layers on a conglomerate bed at its base. The Sespe formation includes
Sespe red sandstone, the namesake of at least one Santa Paula cat. The
language of its sedimentary structures sounds a geological poetry:
"cross bedding, graded bedding, rhythmic bedding, convolute bedding, scour channels, ripple marks and load casts" (45). The report
suggests the Sespe formation to be of continental origin, evidenced by
the absence of marine fossils and the presence of fossil land animals.

By this time in your walk, the trail will play games with your mind.
Just as you glimpse your destination not far down the canyon, you
will veer away with the mountainside. This will happen several times,
and you will walk much farther than you expect. However, if you
stick with it, your spirits will rise as you look back up Tar Creek to
see—if it is spring and there is sufficient runoff—the creek's blue-
green water plunging over a succession of sandstone lips into clear,
teacup pools. Each teacup pours into the next until finally the creek
levels out only to leap sixty feet to its death among the boulders at its
confluence with Sespe Creek.

The waterfall ledge suggests the Coldwater formation, which begins just below the level at which the Mel Blanc oil well ends. Composed of green-gray, white, or reddish brown sandstone, this Eocene
formation forms the dramatic, hoodooish ribs of stone common

above the banks of Sespe Creek. As the report puts it, "Erosion of these strata has produced hogbacks where the beds are steeply dipping, and cliffs where the beds are lying flat" (45). Having followed switchbacks down to Sespe Creek, you will now want to rest and have lunch next to the stream among massive boulders of both Sespe and Coldwater origin. Your walk back up the trail will mirror the more direct but less scenic route oil takes up the Mel Blanc well.

The use of petroleum in the Sespe dates back to its first human residents. The Chumash dug asphalt from natural seeps and used it to seal baskets, bind yucca fibers together for paint brushes, and provide foundations for shell inlays (Rintoul 1). One "artifact"—a twenty-three-foot plank canoe held together with dowels and plant fiber and sealed with asphalt—was built in 1914 by Fernando Librado Kitsepawit. This was the same man who told the ethnographer J. P. Harrington so much about Chumash life; he was probably 110 years old when he built the boat two years before his death.

Immigrants to California also found practical uses for petroleum. Up north, asphalt was used to grease log skids in timber country and to pave sidewalks in San Francisco, where it sold for thirty dollars a ton (Rintoul 3). Closer to the Sespe, the Stanford brothers and Hayward Coleman began tunneling into Sulphur Mountain north of Santa Paula in 1865 in an experiment to extract crude oil (Rintoul 4). They drove tunnels upward as far as four hundred feet, inventing a water-blast method to force fresh air into the tunnels. Oil and water drained out in gutters to holding tanks. Tunnels were also used in Wheeler Canyon at the western edge of what is now the Sespe Wilderness. The crude oil from these operations was hauled by wagon to Ventura and from there by ship to San Francisco where it was distilled into lamp and lubricating oils.

The first productive well in what came to be the Sespe field was completed in 1887. It produced 185 barrels a day (Dosch 41). By 1900, the various areas of the oil field held between sixty and seventy producing wells operated by numerous companies. Since the rugged country made road building extremely difficult, rail tramways were often used to transport men and equipment to otherwise inaccessible drill sites. The production of many wells was initially high, before tapering off dramatically within a couple of years. Over the next few decades, the growth of the oil field was fairly slow, due partly to the production realities, but also to the rough landscape and the incendiary nature of chaparral ecology. In 1917, a fire started in Hopper Canyon in what is now a national wildlife refuge. The fire came over the hill into the Tar Creek and Topatopa areas of the oil field and trapped oil workers and their families as it destroyed twenty wooden derricks, houses, tanks, and a gas plant (41). Three women and a child who tried to escape to the creek were killed. One worker reclined in a small depression and covered himself with loose shale as the fire burned over him. He lived.

The production of the Sespe Oil Field began to rise in the late 1960s, near the beginning of Day's career, with the discovery of the lower portion of the Basal Sespe zone (43). At about this same time, companies reinvigorated production by fracturing the zones into which the wells drilled. Fracturing is accomplished by introducing various substances into the well under pressure to expand the subterranean spaces into which oil can seep. Roughnecks pump down everything from nylon balls and sand-oil mixes to glass beads and walnut shells—anything that stands up to pressures of up to seven thousand pounds per square inch. Day tells me that the Sespe has been "sand-fracked" about as much as it can be. It seems the oil field is gradually winding down.

The numbers bear this out. In the 1980s the Sespe Oil Field produced around 1.3 million barrels of oil annually. By 1992, production dropped below one million barrels and has steadily declined since. The totals for 2001 were 405,335 barrels of oil and 1,072,102 billion cubic feet of natural gas. The cumulative totals since the inception of the field are about 47 million barrels of oil and 60 billion cubic feet of gas.

Despite the meagerness of what's left, the Sespe, as part of the larger Los Padres National Forest, is part of the Bush administration's efforts to expand oil and gas leases on federal lands. The U.S. Forest Service is drafting a plan that will identify areas in the Los Padres acceptable for future leasing, even though oil companies have not lately shown interest. So far, the parts of the Los Padres that show the most potential are the Cuyama Valley northwest of the Sespe, Piedra Blanca near the headwaters of Sespe Creek, and the Sespe Oil Field. According to Forest Service estimates, 74 percent of the 140,000 acres potentially available for lease in the Los Padres lies within "Inventoried Roadless Areas." In slightly less bureaucratic terms, this is potential designated wilderness. Beneath this ground lies perhaps 84 million barrels of oil—about one percent of total U.S. reserves. Since transportation in the United States consumes about 20 million barrels per day, the entire Los Padres reserves would drive us for four days plus a few hours.

The timing of the leasing proposal is strange, since a major revision of the entire management plan for the Los Padres National Forest is under way and due to be completed in 2004. Part of this revision process has included public hearings throughout the region where local residents can voice their opinions about the value and purpose of the national forest. Why not wait for the whole picture to be outlined before deciding on the place of oil and gas development? The U.S. Forest Service claims that the 1980 Energy Security Act requires that leases be processed "notwithstanding the current status of any plan." This has been upheld in court. The existence of such a backward statute recalls the notorious 1872 Mining Act, which also holds public lands and democratic processes hostage to a history of frontier exploitation and to the few who wish to continue to get a free ride.

The debate over oil in the Los Padres makes California seem like a microcosm of the whole country. Already, oil association officials are suggesting that any new exploration is good and can help increase California's energy independence. The electricity crisis of the summer of 2001 is held up as example A, even though Californians demonstrated the amazing potential of conservation and restraint to answer such crises. On the national level, we hear that the Arctic National Wildlife Refuge must be drilled to increase our "national energy security," although the refuge might provide the United States with only a six-month fix ten years down the road. Slightly increased fuel efficiency could save much more than this. The statistics don't seem to make sense except from the perspective of addiction. But even addicts can sometimes recognize their own trail to nowhere. So who benefits? Well, the dealers do.

If you take a half-step away from the billions that could be made by oil companies to look at the big picture, this destruction for the sake of a relatively short buzz of a joyride doesn't make sense. Why don't we just start the twelve-step process now and have some birds to listen to as we come out of the DT's? A simple-minded question, perhaps. In my more cynical moments, I wonder if there may be more going on here than a story about oil. After all, the Los Padres is not alone in being targeted for "resource development." Oil and gas exploration is gathering momentum on federal lands in the backcountry of Utah, Wyoming, and all along the Rocky Mountain Front. But you don't hear much about it. While the celebrity spokespeople and e-mail campaigns focus on the photogenic arctic caribou herds, exploratory roads are being carved into the wilds. In the Los Padres as elsewhere, the lease areas correspond to roadless areas that have been proposed as additions to official wilderness and wild and scenic river. Even if the exploration doesn't lead to drilling and production, the roads will be left. Off-roaders will find them and claim "rights" to recreation. Habitat will be lost. Potential wilderness will be erased before it even gets on the books. This may be the point as much as the oil.

The Cuyama Valley may be more at risk than the Sespe, but there are connections between the two places. Condors regularly fly from Hopper Mountain over Piedra Blanca to the foraging areas of the Cuyama and to Lion Canyon where some of them were released. Over nine hundred acres of their designated critical habitat fall within potentially high-yield lease areas. The condor, remember, is just the headliner for the twenty-three species currently listed as endangered and threatened in the Los Padres.

All this makes me reconsider my experiences in the oil field. At first glance, the Sespe Oil Field seems to present a compelling example of recovery and resistance to human intrusion. In "God's Grandeur," the poet Gerard Manley Hopkins writes, "all is seared with trade; bleared, smeared with toil . . . / And for all this nature is never spent; / There lives the dearest freshness deep down things." Here in the Sespe, the landscape tears itself down, burns itself over, and grows itself back to life. Humans etch scars that seem to fade with time. But I wonder, as always, how to know what has been lost or how to estimate what would have been. I wonder if the Sespe's resistance and re-creation is more than just appearance and if so, whether the Sespe is unique. What is true in the Sespe may not be in the arctic tundra. It may not even be true in the Cuyama Valley just a few mountains over.

I tag along as Day makes his afternoon rounds looking for irregularities. We stop at one pad where he explains how gas-traps separate crude oil from the natural gas and send each down its own pipeline. At the final holding tank for the oil, he shows me the heater treater that warms the oil to reduce its water content before it enters a huge storage tank that holds all the oil from this part of the Sespe field. From the tank, oil flows down a pipeline to Fillmore. The companies get paid based on gauges that look like little slow seismographs charting the flow through the main pipeline and accounting for various levels of water content. In between the technical explanations, Day tells me stories of the best and worst of times on the mountain.

Up until the early 70s, he says, the cowboys from the Hopper Ranch would invite the oil workers over for a big barbecue after the annual roundup. "We'd eat steaks and start drinking and end up staying overnight at the ranch and going straight to work the next morning." Some of the stories return to the wildlife: "I remember when condors were just another bird. They were fun to see, but they didn't mean that much back then."

"There used to be a lot more grassland up here," says Day as he looks over the hillside. "Now there's so much brush you can't get through it. A burn would be the best thing that could happen to this land. It would be good for the plants and animals. They come back fast. But we'd go through hell with mudslides the next time it rained."

Rain and washouts sometimes made work in the oil field an adventure. "One year, a big storm came in, and everybody on the mountain met down at the ranger station on the main road at 1 P.M. We had two skip loaders, and it took us until 10:30 that night to get to Fillmore. We'd clear out the road, get two or three cars through, and it would fill back in again. Nobody got hurt." Day describes what it was like when the El Nino weather pattern dumped an unusual amount of rain on California a few years ago. "The main flow line broke in a landslide," he says. "All the roads were washed out, so a helicopter pilot dropped me off at each pad to shut things down. He'd drop us right down between trees and power lines, then rev the thing up for take-off. The whole machine would shake like it was going to fall apart, and up we'd go. It was kind of nice to get to see the country from up high like that."

The surviving roads in the oil field are often dramatic, clinging to the sides of hills and switching back so steeply you have to take turns wide just to get around. Day pointed out roads he had helped to build that are now little more than a slight horizontal leveling on an otherwise plunging, brush-covered mountainside. All it takes is a bit of neglected maintenance. He tells me of driving down to Sespe Creek in the 1960s to go fishing after work. Day calls the area along the Sespe at the base of the trail "Green Cabins," though the cabins that housed oil workers no longer exist and the name doesn't appear on maps. Drilling in the area began in 1901 and ended by 1954. When the wells were abandoned, Sikorski Sky Crane helicopters were used to haul people and equipment to and from the rugged site (Rintoul 146). Still, in 1994, a U.S. Forest Service ranger found an old leaky tank containing 1,700 gallons of crude. The tank was brittle and irreparable, so workers manually transferred the oil to 33-gallon drums that could be flown out by helicopter. The oil was processed to offset some of the costs of the operation.

The first time I ventured down the Tar Creek trail—the same one Day drove decades ago—I got a late start and wasn't sure how wise it was to continue. Then I walked around the next switchback and there, scratched in the dirt in four-foot block letters: GOD KNOWS! I stared at the words for a moment, feeling comforted, relieved, embarrassed, and guilty all at once. But I kept going. Later, I missed a turn in a boulder-choked wash and worked my way toward the base of the big waterfall near the confluence of Tar Creek and the Sespe. After lunch on a house-size rock near the fall, I realized I'd lost track of where I had emerged from the brush. I picked a path at random and started climbing. It was hot and dusty. I brushed ticks from my sleeves. I slipped and fell through poison oak. I lost a sandal that had been strapped to my pack and threw its mate down the slope as a reward for the next wayward soul. Why do I put myself through this, I wondered? God knows.

Last fall, my friend Mike and I backpacked down the Tar Creek trail and upstream along the Sespe. We missed no turns, but it was still rough going. The brush above the creek bed was impenetrable and unstable, and the creek itself was a maze of boulders and pools. Occasionally, we would pass natural tar seeps where the inky goo collected in sandstone depressions. Sometimes the tar would ooze slowly into the creek where it would float away in fragments and leave a rainbow slick on the surface. Small arroyo toads hopped around the edges of the seeps and dove through the slicks to the bottom of the streambed. To make the rock scrambling easier, we ditched our packs at a good campsite before continuing upstream. After a while, we fought up the bank through the riparian brush and found a grown-in trail, sections of which were paved with asphalt. In the middle of the trail rested the translucent skin of a rattlesnake. The pavement seemed unlikely and out of place, along with the remains of a wooden wheel centered by a heavy iron gear. Sections of pipe and rusting metal oil tanks were almost invisible in the thick brush. If we had stayed in the creek bed, we wouldn't have noticed any of these items. We were surrounded by human history, but the evidence was almost imperceptible.

By the time we packed up the next morning, it was warm, so we stopped to swim in a clear pool. We dove over and over from a big rock, and I put on goggles to watch trout or steelhead swim around in the shadows. Before too long I felt chilled to the bone, and I lay down wrapped in sun and radiating sandstone. The pool had seemed clear enough, but I still found my skin smeared by small brown splotches.

Before starting up the Tar Creek trail, we tried to find the road that crosses Sespe Creek on the topo maps. This would have been where Jim Day said he often drove a truck across the stream if the water was low enough. After beating the brush and bouldering for a half hour, we found nothing. It was gone without a trace.

Everywhere, the landscape seemed to be erasing the marks people have made upon it. Inscriptions like roads and trails are the first to go.

Metal and iron artifacts persist, but disappear under landslides and burnished buckwheat flowers gone to seed. It almost seemed that if we stood still long enough, we too would fade into the landscape. Take a nap and you're history. I'm still not sure what to make of this observation. Is this reason for optimism about the ultimately ephemeral impact people have on diverse, functioning ecosystems? Is it a precious exception? Or is it an illusion altogether?

CHAPTER 7

Forgive Us Our Trespasses

Steelhead Habitat

*The sight of these massive, mountain-born, faithfully returning
ocean travelers in a clear flow before me . . . feels like some impossibly literal answer to an unspoken prayer. Words aren't needed in
the presence of such an answer.*

—DAVID JAMES DUNCAN,
"Salmon's Second Coming"

For years I never mentioned this to anyone, and I feel a little uncomfortable writing about it now. A wise man once said prayer is best kept
private, away from public display. Still, prayer is the beginning of my
feeling for fish.

I attended a church some years ago south of downtown Los Angeles that was very generous and patient with its silences. Occasionally,
these liturgical spaces could be, ironically, disquieting. The length of
the quiet varied depending on who was running the service, and after
a "normal" period passed, some people would glance around, wondering whether someone had missed a cue. Mostly, though, the silences allowed for the practice of mindfulness. This was not the type
of meditation that encouraged an escape from the too-much-with-us
world, for as often as not there were police helicopters overhead or
sirens from the fire station down the street. Even on Sunday morn-
ings.

In this place, in the company of people diverse in every way imaginable, in the heart of a city occasionally torn by natural disasters, police corruption, and racial tension, I found myself thinking of salmon. Over and over, salmon would swim up the stream of my consciousness and spawn thoughts of themselves. I would will chinook smolts safely downstream through the turbines of hydroelectric dams. In the ocean, I would evade orcas, sea lions, and fishermen. I would imagine the cold mountain headwaters calling us home, and with the rest I would strain against the current over fish ladders and waterfalls and through too-warm reservoirs infused with the chemicals of farms and factories. For years, I filled Sunday silences with prayers for fish. This was the closest thing to a spiritual discipline I've ever been able to maintain, other than walking or paddling.

As I think back, I can begin to understand why I dreamed of fish in the city. I was longing for wholeness and completion, for cycles that made sense. I needed to contemplate a perfect image of transformation and resurrection in a city in need of such things. This was a time in Los Angeles of urban insurrection, cataclysmic fires and floods, and literal earth shattering. Brenda and I were trying to make a home in an unfamiliar and unstable city at the edge of the continent. In the Mediterranean climate and successive apartments in endless rows of apartment buildings, my body, newly arrived from the Great Lakes, felt disoriented and unable to sense the seasons. I peered through sun and smog for hawks and crows over the freeways. I heard opossums in the shrubs at night, and listened closely to the yipping of coyotes. I saw fish backlit through waves while I bodysurfed at Venice Beach. I watched brown pelicans dive after them, harassed all the while by seagulls. But such natural survivals seemed exceptions rather than signs of connection and integrity. I was learning, as I still am, to see traces of hope.

And it helped to think of salmon and steelhead at least once a week. It seemed to me—from both scientific and spiritual points of view—that if the world were right for salmon, it would be right for most other things as well. They were an indicator species, a sign of the ties that bind. The power of this sign was confirmed for me when, during this same period in my life, my family gathered for Christmas on Vancouver Island, and I saw for the first time dead and nearly dead salmon lining the banks of a creek. They had spawned, and in decomposition they bestowed their final gift to the next generation of salmon and to the land. In their end was a beginning. It all seemed wonderfully poetic, if somewhat malodorous.

However, there were limitations in attempting to deal with the stresses of a new and intense place by envisioning real but symbolic creatures in ecosystems half a continent away. Like most Southern California residents, I didn't know steelhead existed nearby, now or ever. I tended to associate spawning fish with Northern California and the Pacific Northwest. In my mind's eye, the fish swam upstream on foggy, drizzly days, resting under cedar snags in deep, cold eddies. They spawned in the shadows of temperate rain forests not yet logged. Arid Southern California with its sporadic stream flows didn't fit my salmonid stereotype.

And as I think on it now, Southern California didn't fit my spiritual stereotypes either. As a place, it did not seem capable of sustaining the sort of wholeness and integrity I wanted to become a part of. I had hoped for a communal sense of identity linked to place and to the wild. But Los Angeles seemed disconnected from itself and its landscape as it worked hard to address the usual set of urban problems: police brutality, distrust and violence between races and neighborhoods, sharp juxtapositions between poverty and wealth. Where the wildness of fire, torrential rain, debris flow, drought, and earthquake intertwined with culture, the city saw more battles to be fought. Natural extremes made natural subtleties seem irrelevant. Nature seemed apart from the concerns of real life. Other places were part of ecosystems and watersheds. Los Angeles seemed beyond all that. It was too far gone. Wholeness here didn't seem conceivable. This, of course, was a misperception.

And so, for spiritual sustenance tied to a sense of place, I turned elsewhere. Like so many others, I spent time at the ocean, surfing or just sitting with my back to the city at sunset. Brenda and I drove to the famous neighboring desert places and to the Sierra Nevada and beyond. I came back from these adventures refreshed, with a longer list of places I would live if I could choose freely. It took some time for me to think of Los Angeles as home, and in the process of that shift, I felt a tug on the line and began to reel in the distant symbols. Closer to home, the fish became more than symbolic. I learned that many of the local streams I hiked along were historic (and even present!) steelhead habitat: Malibu Creek, Topanga Creek, Corral Creek, the Ventura River, Matilija Creek, the Santa Clara River, and Sespe Creek. The flowing waters became alive with possibility.

Sometimes, among boulders tumbled from cliffs, I've strapped on swim goggles and slowly immersed myself in the gentle current of calm Sespe pools. After a few deep breaths, I'll duck under to enter a weightless world of slow sound and refraction. The fingerlings that earlier scattered as my shadow crossed the water from shore now calmly keep their distance. They cease their darting and fin the water cautiously. Steelhead may still be a reality in Sespe Creek. They may be one strand in the remarkable web linking the ocean with the creek, the lowlands with the high country, human population centers with the places that sustain all manner of life. They are part of what makes the Sespe wild, and they are no less fish for being excellent metaphors.

To understand the value of steelhead in both idea and reality, it helps to turn to habitat and genetics, for the southern steelhead is unique among steelhead.

Though I grew up in Michigan saying "steelhead salmon," and still hear the phrase occasionally, it is not entirely accurate. Though steelhead (*Oncorhynchus mykiss*) are members of the salmonid family, they are really rainbow trout that live through a cycle similar to that of salmon. That is, they are anadromous. They hatch and grow in freshwater streams before migrating toward the ocean as juveniles. After adjusting to salt water in a tidal estuary, they strike out to sea to spend a few years putting on weight. Eventually, they return to the streams to spawn in clean water flowing over gravel. Unlike the salmon I saw along the creek in British Columbia, steelhead don't necessarily die after reproducing. Adult steelhead, having spawned, may turn around and head downstream to complete the cycle again.

This cycle of steelhead life replenishes watersheds all along the Pacific Coast north to Alaska. Yet of all the steelhead in all these streams, the southern steelhead is distinct as a result of its difficult habitat. Once a resident of streams from San Francisco to northern Baja California, the southern steelhead has adapted to the variable, small stream flows and warm water temperatures typical of Southern California. Consider Malibu Creek, which flows from its estuary into the sea a stone's throw north of the surf break made famous by Gidget movies in the 1960s. Like most Southern California streams, Malibu Creek's temperatures are often above the levels normally thought to be highly stressful to steelhead. If your knowledge of steelhead came from the north, you wouldn't expect these fish to survive. The fish, however, don't seem to mind. A residency of thousands of years has allowed the southern steelhead to adapt to the only available conditions.

In addition to adapting to warm temperatures, southern steelhead must also deal with stream flows that peak much later and for a much shorter time than those of rivers in wetter climates to the north. The southern steelhead will congregate in estuaries and near the mouths of streams waiting for spring freshets to fill the streambeds. But even then, streams often flow too fast and violently for the fish to swim upstream, and the fish must wait still longer to catch the flow as it tapers off. A fish caught midswim by floods may temporarily use smaller tributaries to escape the peak flow. Its challenging habitat has caused the southern steelhead to become a very persistent, patient, and hardy fish.

But what if the stream doesn't flow at all? After all, it is not unusual for drought conditions in Southern California to persist for many consecutive years. The steelhead answer, arrived at through time and natural selection, is to seek deep pools and to survive even for several years in freshwater, waiting for the next chance to head out to sea. Steelhead retain this crucial adaptation through interbreeding with inland rainbow trout, which are genetically identical. Likewise, biologists have observed, inland rainbows will become anadromous when given the opportunity.

Geneticists suggest that the southern steelhead's mitochondrial DNA reflects its adaptations to a challenging habitat and that the fish carries more genetic diversity than steelhead to the north. The southern steelhead may, therefore, be the evolutionary ancestor of all steel-head populations. The theory goes like this: Since, it is presumed, fish can't live under ice, the glaciers of the last ice age wiped out inland and coastal species. However, the ancestors of today's fish survived in the Gulf of California as the glaciers melted into the Colorado River watershed. As the ice receded, some trout migrated up the Colorado River to populate the Rocky Mountain and Great Basin streams. Fish that migrated around the tip of Baja California gradually repopulated streams northward along the Pacific coast as they became available. The southern steelhead, therefore, has resided in its habitat longer than other populations and represents a precious genetic legacy.

But the southern steelhead is in trouble. In the whole of California, steelhead populations have declined by over 90 percent since 1950. In Southern California there has been a 99 percent decline since the turn of the twentieth century. The populations of at least twenty-three streams that have historically supported steelhead are extinct.

This dramatic decline in numbers is the result of a host of factors mostly involving habitat. Many rivers and streams near urban areas have been "channelized," that is, cemented in for flood control. A channelized stream has no boulders, tree roots, meanders, or eddies to slow down the flow and allow a steelhead to work its way upstream. A channelized stream has little vegetative cover to cool and hide fish. Above the cement channels, sediment from agricultural and residential development has buried many of the gravel beds the fish need to spawn. Runoff into streams may contain industrial and agricultural wastes.

One reason for steelhead decline, and perhaps the most important factor in their recovery, is that they often face barriers between the ocean and their spawning and rearing habitat inland. A barrier may be as simple as an old culvert under the Pacific Coast Highway that drops ten feet into a jumble of rocks on the beach. Or, the barrier may be a silted-in dam that has long ceased to fulfill any role in gathering water or preventing floods. In addition to cutting steelhead off from their best spawning and rearing habitat, these barriers have separated anadromous fish from inland populations. This artificial condition has led to a struggle between the National Marine Fisheries Service, which is responsible for sea-run steelhead, and Fish and Wildlife, which manages inland fish. The result is that NMFS currently refuses to acknowledge the crucial tie between the anadromous and inland populations and to designate critical habitat upstream of dams and south of Malibu Creek. NMFS thereby avoids the political difficulties of designating critical habitat in urban areas and those areas that developers wish to make urban. A coalition of environmental groups has sued the agencies to force them to act on the best available science and to follow the law. Speaking solely of fish, one biologist who has conducted extensive habitat surveys used a phrase that suggests a similarity between success in spawning and effectiveness in politics: "It's all about access."

The political scene is complicated by the hazy distinction between anadromous steelhead and resident inland trout. In places where the two potentially mix, it's nearly impossible to tell one from the other. Usually those returning from the sea-smorgasbord are clearly bulkier and longer than resident inland trout. In Southern California, though, even small steelhead return to spawn, perhaps because conditions somehow favor small fish. This sometimes leads to anecdotal steelhead sightings—an angler may catch the biggest trout he's ever seen in the river and immediately thinks steelhead. He may be right, but the fish may also be the biggest rainbow trout in the river, having never finned seawater. A survey in Sespe Creek once turned up one eighteen-inch fish whose scale readings indicated steelhead and another eighteen-inch fish whose scale readings indicated trout. The more sophisticated distinguishing technique of analyzing strontium-calcium ratios in fish seems to work well on steelhead in Oregon but has proven unreliable in Southern California.

Ultimately, steelhead and inland trout might best be thought of as the same species living two different life histories. Fish from a particular hatch in a particular stream might go either way, depending on a myriad of factors so complex in their interactions as to defy understanding. You might as well flip a coin.

Although sea-run steelhead and inland trout are genetically identical, and although the resident trout could become seed populations for steelhead runs if barriers were removed, only the steelhead currently receives protection under the Endangered Species Act. On the face of it, this doesn't make sense. Why not protect all the fish that could help lead to the recovery of the species? Furthermore, the limited ESA protection takes an easier political path by avoiding designating controversial critical habitat and allowing anglers upstream of dams to continue to catch rainbow trout, which, viewed separately, are thriving. Some biologists, however, argue that limiting ESA protection just to oceangoing fish is not such a bad thing. They worry that listing inland trout populations as endangered would make their management and recovery work more complicated and difficult. Some have also suggested that including inland trout would boost trout/steelhead numbers to levels where those working to gut the ESA could claim the species is no longer endangered or even threatened.

Despite the legal and political complexities of steelhead recovery, our institutions have still not caught up with the variable life histories of the fish itself. The fish recognizes that in the variable coastal streams of a drought-prone region, it's best to hedge your bets and keep your options open. The very inconsistency that may make possible the steelhead's recovery is hard to account for from a human perspective and time line.

One U.S. Forest Service biologist says, "Those fish went to places you would never believe there were fish. There seems to be something in their genetics that makes them want to go further, to keep repopulating" (Finney and Edmondson 11). They are survivors. They are adaptive. They will recolonize good habitat if barriers are removed. Resident rainbows might begin to live like steelhead in restored, free-flowing streams. These are natural reasons for hope.

There is also some good habitat left. Though it may be the ultimate test of bioregional imagination to think of steelhead spurring the revitalization of the urban rivers, Sespe Creek is closer to reality. The Sespe flows freely through protected wilderness. In its upper reaches and its dozens of tributaries, the Sespe offers textbook habitat—clear, clean water, gravel spawning beds, and deep, protective pools. Only the Vern Freeman Diversion on the Santa Clara—recently equipped with a fish ladder—stands between a Sespe steelhead and the sea.

Which raises an interesting question: why, given the Sespe's quality, protected habitat, are there not more steelhead? The answer may be that the Sespe, though beautiful and wild, is the best of what's left, not the best that ever was. Historical evidence suggests that the Santa Clara River, upstream of its confluence with the Sespe, produced staggering numbers of steelhead. This habitat included the large Piru Creek drainage that wraps around the eastern and northern portions of the Sespe watershed. Piru Creek now flows into two reservoirs and is a dead stream as far as steelhead are concerned. The Santa Clara itself has numerous problems. The agricultural fields lining much of its path occasionally produce runoff laced with chemicals and sediment. Newhall Ranch, a proposed 22,000-house development on the banks of the Santa Clara, will require that portions of the river and its tributaries be channelized. An invasive, non-native, bamboolike grass called arundo constricts its path to the sea, and millions of dollars will be needed to try to eradicate it.

It may be that even in the best of times Sespe Creek contributed only a relatively small percentage of the Santa Clara's steelhead. Perhaps some fish reared in the Santa Clara and in Piru Creek ended up spawning in the Sespe, helping to keep its population healthy. On its own, even a stream as impressive as the Sespe is diminished.

There are also cultural reasons for hope. The best news may be the emergence of the Southern California Steelhead Coalition, whose member organizations represent over a quarter million people. Only a few years ago, group representatives met in loosely organized meetings to consider whether such a diverse coalition would even be possible and to try to gauge what effects it might have. In the last two years, however, the coalition has accomplished a number of remarkable goals. It has consolidated a strong voice in favor of steelhead and has placed representatives on important state legislative advisory committees. As a result, some of the steelhead recovery funding that usually flows north has begun to be redirected south toward the fish many people overlook. The coalition has also lobbied the Department of Fish and Game to hire biologists devoted to the southern steelhead. At the same time, coalition members are working on sophisticated habitat analyses, beginning on-the-ground restoration projects, and educating Southern Californians about the unique qualities of the fish in their local streams.

At a recent coalition meeting the atmosphere was one of celebration mixed with creative tension. Coalition members watched presentations of habitat analysis come to fruition, but carefully worded questions hinted at areas of ongoing debate—the appropriateness of captive rearing smolts, which watersheds should receive priority, whether ESA listing should extend to inland trout. Still, it was clear the coalition provides an important bridge between different agencies and organizations. In person and through e-mail, people get together and talk about what they all care about, even if they care in different ways.

As an educator, not a fish biologist, I see the coalition as a sign and an instrument of how southern steelhead can grow in the minds of Southern Californians as they do in our streams. On one hand, this awareness is crucial to providing the grassroots support to fund restoration projects and protect watersheds. More subtly, steelhead can make a difference in the life and culture of the region. They can swim up the stream of our collective consciousness to help us think in new ways about where and how we live.

I've seen this process begin when I've presented slide shows explaining the connections between habitat and genetics and outlining what stands in the way of healthy local steelhead runs. Kids at a Griffith Park science magnet school gawked when I showed them photos of arm-long, fat steelhead caught in the Los Angeles River in the 1930s a few hundred of yards from where we sat in a darkened classroom. I could see and hear them reevaluating the river they crossed daily and regarded as dead thing. Thinking of steelhead sparked for them a new understanding of home. The reality of the past brought hope for the future. It also made them reconsider their actions in the present. Others had preached to them that litter and waste from the streets flows first to the river and then to the ocean. But to a kid in North Hollywood, the river can seem abstract and the ocean far away. In steelhead, however, there was a vision of the river— even the Los Angeles River—as living water.

I've seen adults register the same amazement, even lifelong residents. Unlike the California condor, the steelhead has faded from the consciousness of Southern Californians. But if an ugly, bald-headed carrion eater can become a wilderness icon, why not a sleek, strong, silvery union of muscle and instinct? Why couldn't the steelhead's life history and remarkable adaptation to its home become a symbol of regeneration and of the bond between upstream and down, urban places and wilderness? There is risk to these metaphors, though. What does it mean to place so much hope on a species in decline? What is the risk to our collective psyche to put our hearts on the line? What do we risk if we don't?

As I think back to my first prayers for salmon and steelhead, I can see that they were tinged with mourning for what has been broken in and between the world and me. I'm not sure I thought of it this way at the time, but in some way I was confessing what ought to be on the lips of all of us in these times of extinction and loss: forgive us our trespasses. Confession is a good start, but it's not the end. Now I know that there are others thinking similar things about steelhead, whether or not they would call these thoughts prayer. What's more, things are getting done. Collectively, we are beginning to see streams from the perspective of steelhead and to make those streams more hospitable. Literal mountains were moved to put up dams and rearrange river bottoms; I'm beginning to have the faith that political, financial, and cultural mountains will move to restore things to a semblance of wholeness. The work of restoration is the work of reconciliation. It looks to me like the work of scientists, activists, and lawyers has deep, spiritual import.

A few steelhead still grace our streams. They could be the beginning of everything.

CHAPTER 8

Scouting

To Boat or Not To Boat

Good judgment comes from experience. Experience comes from bad judgment. —UNKNOWN

"You gotta do it. Maybe not now, maybe not this year, but you gotta do it." The voice held the steady calm of one who has seen beyond, deep into the heart of things. Chris Nybo, one of the very few who regularly kayaks Sespe Creek, was trying—and failing—to offer balanced advice on whether I should attempt to paddle the Sespe myself. Occasionally, his honest appraisal of the hazards would break into eloquent descriptions of the "inner sanctum" of the Sespe. He calls the creek one of the premier wilderness kayaking runs in the western United States. Long pause. "You gotta do it."

Now I'm trying to decide for myself. It's a sunny afternoon in May, and I'm scrambling my way up Sespe Creek while Brenda lounges on a rock imprinted by fossil shells. We've hiked down Tar Creek, the only trail that descends into the canyon upstream from Fillmore. I've come here to read the water. I want to know what I might be in for.

After squeezing through a passage under a boulder the size of my garage, I get a good look at a stretch of water that causes me, as kayakers say, to pucker. My innards do Eskimo rolls as I watch the creek sweep through successive tight drops between huge boulders past undercut rocks waiting to suck down a slightly misplaced boater. In the standard scale of whitewater difficulty—from flatwater class I to deathwater class VI—this is clearly very technical class V. American Whitewater describes class V as having "extremely long, obstructed or very violent rapids which expose a paddler to added risk." A class V river may have large, unavoidable holes, congested chutes, and infrequent eddies. "Scouting is recommended but may be difficult. Swims are dangerous, and rescue is often difficult even for experts."

Downstream from the boulder-choked drops, the creek braids into three strands, each with rock sieves. The size of the boulders makes it impossible to see the routes entirely, and there's no clear indication which line, if any, is runnable. OK. Let's say I carry around this section. I look upstream and down, and everything I see looks nearly as difficult. A long, brutal carry. I try to imagine hauling a loaded kayak around, over, and through this maze of boulders and house rocks. A tired paddler facing such a portage might just say the hell with it—I'll take my chances in the water. I sigh. The river is speaking to me, but I'm also speaking to myself. You don't gotta do it. Not this year.

Such is the process of scouting. One doesn't always find what one wants. But even when the river and my inner voice speak their clear, "We think not," I still listen closely for contradictory whispers. I've studied water since I was a kid, decades before I thought to take up kayaking. I would wander beside streams, tracing a watercourse to predict the route of a small twig through the hazards. Finding a suitable stick, I would toss it into the stream and run beside it until an eddy pulled it from the main current. Then I would do it again. If the stream was large enough I would heave logs as heavy as I could lift. Yet I could be just as fascinated by yellow, canoe-shaped willow leaves in a rivulet. I would watch log or leaf carefully until I learned to intuit the different courses taken by each. I began to sense the relationship flowing between the stream and chance.

Now, as a whitewater paddler, I've renewed my study of flow and possibility. Like all boaters, I scout, which is to say I stand alongside a river and paddle it in my mind to decide whether or how to do it in body. I imagine peeling out of the eddy and slipping down the tongue at the top of a rapid, maybe trying to catch and surf the first green wave. Blown off the wave, I flow toward the rock midrapid and imagine the strokes I need to swing into the eddy behind it just above a sticky hole. I visualize what will happen if I miss that move—the impact and disorientation as I "windowshade" in the hole, the desire for air. I note that the left shoulder of the hole looks escapable if I keep my wits and stay in my boat. Gradually, the river's possibilities become imprinted on my mind as I sense how to move within its currents. If I can't see and feel myself making a necessary move, or if my mouth is so dry I can't spit thinking of the consequences, I know I should consider carrying my kayak around the rapid. I've learned through experience to feel the borderline between helpful adrenaline and debilitating fear. The tingle in my fingers above a drop is a good sign; tightness in the hips is not. But this is just the beginning of the decision.

There are still many questions to be asked. Am I having a good day? Have I been paddling precisely? Am I tired? How much light left today? What's the weather like and how cold is the water? Who am I with and how good are they? Do they have rescue skills and gear?

Just when I think I've made my decision, picked a line or not, perhaps one of my companions will see other possibilities. We might talk it through and compare what we've experienced in our minds' eyes. I concede that sometimes others can be better judges of my skill level than I am. "Of course you can make that move!" they might say. "Remember that drop we did last month? This is no worse . . . except for that ledge hole on river left."

Scouting is mostly about reading water, but it also has to do with understanding connections between your state of mind, your physical responses, and the river. Ultimately, boaters may become exceptionally sensitive to the play between internal and external landscapes. During a shuttle to a put-in last season, a woman told me how just before the 1996 Northridge earthquake she had begun to think of herself as a confident class v boater. After the quake wrecked her house and her psyche, she said fear made it difficult for her to paddle as she once had. I know her to be a steady, solid paddler, but years later she is still not sure she'll ever make it back to where she once was. She, like the rest of us, watches the water and looks deep inside.

This process of scouting is part of what I love about kayaking. It pairs serious analysis with seeing the stream creatively as a child would. It's an excuse to imagine you are the willow leaf or the stick tumbling with the current, then spinning quietly at the bottom of the rapid. I think most kayakers find that scouting becomes an unbreakable habit even where actually running a rapid is an impossibility. We'll look for a line in Niagara Falls or in the rush along a street gutter in a rainstorm. We're like surfers describing a tidal wave or a perfectly shaped three-inch point break at the edge of an inland lake. I've found myself standing above the foam and spray of unrunnable class VI rapids, thinking to myself, "If someone put a gun to my head like Kevin Bacon did to Meryl Streep in the movie *The River Wild,* I'd try to boof that rock center right, dig out of the recirculation, work left away from the undercut, use the pillow to slip past the fang rock, take a deep breath for the mystery move, and hope that last hole sucks me deep enough to squirt me out along the bottom of the river." A little part of me wishes someone would step out from the bushes with a revolver and say, "Run that thar river, mister," because, well, it almost looks doable. There would be a certain release and relaxation in having no choice.

But boaters usually do have choices. Most of us choose not to run certain rapids or rivers. Sometimes this is an easy decision. We recognize water we want no part of. Ever. Other times, though, a river tugs at our hearts even as our heads tell us, "No, no, no." We hear it calling, and we can't help but listen. We see other paddlers run it repeatedly and arrive at the take-out with sparkling eyes and tangled tongues. They give up trying to tell how it was and just shake their heads and grin. We begin to think we may have the skills, stamina, and mindset to survive, but we're not quite sure. We mutter the first rule of kayak safety: Do Not Die. And still the river calls.

Sespe Creek does this to me. So far, I've resisted, but it hasn't been easy. I know enough of the Sespe to know the beauty that must await those who flow at its pace. I've stood where hiking trails end and watched the creek disappear around a bend in a jumble of house-size boulders. In my mind's eye I've seen bear tracks on beaches accessible only from the water and side creeks tumbling over the canyon's rim to join the Sespe.

I also know enough of kayaking to know that water has a unique ability to reorient one's relationship to a place. Some call it "river time." This feeling has to do with the inevitable surrender to forces entirely apart from oneself. It has to do with the intuition that the timelessness of the stream's flow can be understood only in each moment. The water changes everything. Senses intermingle so that the rippling of reflected light on water mimics the canyon wren's cascading call. The smell of wet sandstone recalls its abrasiveness to the skin. Critters that would flee from a hiker wait calmly as you float by. On water I feel conjoined with the entire landscape, even that beyond the riverbanks. I know that paddling the Sespe would deepen my experience and understanding of the landscape. There's a story John Muir tells of climbing Mount Ritter in Yosemite where, in a precarious spot, he froze momentarily before suddenly "life blazed forth again with preternatural clearness. . . . Every rift in the rock was seen as through a microscope, and my limbs moved with a positiveness and precision with which I seemed to have nothing to do at all" (45). And then there's that other story of Muir waking up flat on his back on a granite slab wondering how long he'd been unconscious.

I think of all the stories in which the desire for union with the landscape becomes all-too literal. There's the young Everett Ruess losing himself in the back of beyond of southern Utah and Edward Abbey making a narrow escape after following the pools of Havasu Canyon until he could go neither up nor down. There's Chris McCandless going "into the wild" only to starve beside an Alaskan river. Recently we've been deluged with stories of survival and death in the thin air of the Himalayas and the mountainous seas of perfect storms. Wilderness and adventure literature are full of examples of the demise of the desirous. As much as I feel kinship with these passionate protagonists, I'd like to think I've learned from them to question my own impulses. Still, the

Sespe keeps calling, and the decision to refrain must be remade continually.

Even if I were to boat the Sespe and all were to go well, the trip would involve considerably more than mystical union with nature. It would also be a great deal of hard work. After leaving a vehicle at the take-out in Fillmore, a boating party drives through Santa Paula and Ojai and up into the mountains via highway 33. Since Lion Camp, the usual put-in, has been closed to vehicles to protect breeding habitat of the red-legged frog and arroyo toad, kayakers must carry their boats a mile or so to the creek. Since each forty-five-pound boat is stuffed with sleeping bag, bivy sack, stove, food, and dry clothes, this is no simple stroll.

But once on the water, the run begins benignly. I've often walked the trail that follows the stream for the first fifteen miles, so I know that I would find the first day of the run enjoyable and relatively easy. I've paddled its length a number of times in my mind. When Sespe Creek turns south, however, near the confluence with Alder Creek, the gradient steepens and the boulders get bigger, forming sieves that could pin and drown a boater who misses a stroke or two and fails to make a last-chance eddy. To get from here to Fillmore requires two days of very serious expedition boating, and there are no trails on which to walk out if you reconsider. If you make it to the Tar Creek trail, you might as well keep going. Even the mandatory portages are difficult and risky.

Or so I've heard. The sections of the inner canyon I've seen never fail to bring little adrenaline spikes. My heart rate rises and my fingers tingle. Doubts fill my head. This portion of the creek is why I've backed off for now. Though I suspect I may be able to make most, maybe all, of the necessary moves, I'm not sure I could make so many in a row for two days straight. I'm not sure I could be perfect.

The decision pains me, however, and for now I've taken my consolation in talking with those who've done what I have not. Hearing of the experiences of those who have paddled the Sespe has been part of the process of appraising both the creek and myself. Yet mindful of the possibility that I may never boat the creek, I've been eager to hear beyond the technical information to the experience itself. I want to know how the creek may have changed boaters' perception of the Sespe Wilderness. I listen to their phrasing for hints of how the creek may have changed their self-perception. I know it's too much to hope that the creek might vicariously flow in my blood the way it does theirs, but at this point I have no other hope beyond paddling the creek in my mind.

I begin by going to the source of Sespe kayaking. The first descent of the Sespe was in 1984 by a party of four that included Yvon Chouinard, the pioneer rock climber and founder of the outdoor clothing company Patagonia. Chouinard's innovations in both sport and business have become legendary. From a blacksmith shop in Ventura, he began hammering out pitons and developing climbing protection devices that are now standard equipment in the gear bags of climbers worldwide. By the mid-1970s he had logged many first ascents of climbing routes in well-known places like Yosemite Valley and lesser-known ones like Sespe Gorge. Chouinard started Patagonia in 1972, and the company for years has modeled possibilities for corporate sustainability and environmental responsibility. Many local environmental groups have been helped along by grants from Patagonia. Keep the Sespe Wild, for example, used Patagonia grant money in the late 1980s to fight for the Sespe's wild and scenic river and wilderness designations. Today, Chouinard lives mainly in Ventura, California, with his family, but he seems to get around a great deal. A recent *Surfer's Journal* includes his own write-up of a sail-and-surf trip in the southern Pacific.

I'm to meet Chouinard at the corporate headquarters in Ventura, a few blocks from the surf of an excellent point break. The employees' vehicles in the parking lot bear a collection of outdoor toys—bikes, whitewater kayaks, surf kayaks, sea kayaks, and many surfboards. As I wait in the reception area I watch salesmen in suits grin sheepishly as Patagonia executives greet them in shorts, floral print shirts, and flip-flops. On the walls behind the receptionist hang paintings of Southern California riparian scenes that could be from a number of places along the Sespe. Soon Chouinard shows up in shorts, T-shirt, and flip-flops, and we go to the adjacent café/deli where employees can get organic lunches.

He looks a little sleepy and not entirely enthusiastic about recounting past adventures, but he grins when I ask him how he learned to kayak. I'm interested in how he acquired the skills that allowed him to survive Sespe Creek; I know from experience that for most people kayaking has a steep learning curve. Chouinard says he learned like most people do, from friends. Unlike most people, he compressed years of learning into days. The first day his friends taught him to roll and took him on a class II–III run on the American River. The next day they did a class IV run on the Merced. His third day of kayaking was spent on the Tuolumne River, a classic class V run. "By the end of the day," he laughs, "I had fifteen stitches and a hurt back. I had to pick up a hitchhiker because I couldn't even drive my car. These guys were hard core." I begin to sense his tolerance for risk and discomfort.

Later, by the time Chouinard attempted the Sespe, he and his friends had logged first descents on rivers throughout California, Idaho, Wyoming, and Chile. I can understand how a creek like the Sespe could get lost in the flow of so much adventure. But because I've seen the difficulty of the run, I begin to read through his understatement. When he says, "We had to portage a few places," I picture the house-sized boulders one would have to carry a heavy kayak over, under, and around. When he says, "You had to be able to hit small eddies," I mentally add, "or else." I ask him how, in the midst of boating all over North America and Chile, they thought to do a local creek. "Well," he says, "it was close by and that was nice. We looked at a map and saw the creek came out by Fillmore, so we went for it." "You didn't hike in first to see what you were getting into?" "No, but we scouted blind corners." They took three days in May to complete the run.

To put their trip in perspective, consider that Chouinard and his friends were paddling Perception Dancers, the first popular plastic whitewater kayak. A Dancer is a narrow boat with pointy ends, built for speed in a straight line. At about twelve feet long, its shape is closer to Olympic slalom boats than to either the tiny freestyle boat or the fat creek boat lying in my garage. Its small cockpit was later modified because people kept getting trapped inside and drowning. A Dancer, in almost every way, is the exact opposite of the ideal boat for a creek like the Sespe. But it was about the only option for Chouinard. Today, creek boats are usually seven to nine feet long and shaped with considerable "rocker," the up-curve at both bow and stern, for sharp, quick turns. The ends are wide and bulbous to prevent pinning between rocks beneath the surface, and the cockpits are large and shaped like keyholes to allow for a quick exit if the boat does pin. Their high volume makes for soft but shallow landings from waterfalls. Today's plastic is also much more rigid than that of a Dancer to prevent the boat from wrapping around a rock and trapping a kayaker by the legs. The evolution of boats meant for steep, technical creeks like the Sespe has given kayakers greater maneuverability and safety and a greater margin for error. Chouinard and his party had none of this. They had to hit tiny, must-make eddies in long boats that were not built to turn fast.

Though the achievement of the first descent impresses me much more than it does him, Chouinard becomes more animated as he places the event in a context that means most to him. As he talks, I can see that scouting blind corners was as much a part of the experience as paddling them. He explains, "I'd rather have boated the river than walked it. While kayaking, we saw the river more clearly than a person could while walking it. We were analyzing currents and eddies . . ." He pauses as if at a loss for words, then sums it all up: "I mean, we were alive."

In a short sentence, he reminds me of what I'm missing in choosing not to paddle the Sespe. But he also reminds me that in simply scouting the creek as a paddler I'm experiencing at least a portion of the liveliness that flows from the stream to the human heart.

As we talk, I begin to understand that his goal was not simply to "claim" another river. Rather, the experience itself was what mattered. His whole philosophy of life revolves around process, he says. "The summit is nothing; it's how you climb that matters." To explain this, he refers to the world of business. Gesturing to the café in which we sit, he suggests that traditional cost-benefit analysis would argue that an organic lunch counter or a child care facility might stand in the way of the goal of profits. Chouinard points out, however, that this way of looking at things underestimates the long-term benefits of re-taining loyal, well-trained employees and the short-term expense of training new ones. Emphasizing short-term profits also decreases the likelihood of achieving long-range goals like changing the culture in which business is conducted. Focusing on the goal rather than the process can be detrimental to achieving the goal. To this way of think-ing, running a corporation and making one's way down a difficult river have a great deal in common. In a speech, Chouinard used the metaphor of zen archery. Instead of trying to hit the bull's-eye, you spend years practicing the movements necessary to release an arrow. Finally, when the process becomes mindless, the arrow arrives at the bull's-eye by itself.

As Chouinard describes his philosophy of life and business, it be-comes clear that kayaking the Sespe was part of the process of making his home territory come alive. Climbing the walls of Sespe Gorge, surfing the breaks of Ventura and Santa Barbara, and kayaking Sespe Creek have helped him live fully in his own backyard. Each experi-ence creates the sort of intensity that helps him see deeply and clearly, outside and inside. "I have to live on the edges," he says.

Months after talking with Chouinard, I find myself thinking about him again, and about the relationship between risk and reward. This time it's not about the river, but about the rock. I'm midway through my first multipitch rock climb, on the four-hundred-foot sandstone face of Sespe Gorge, where Chouinard put up a number of routes. Unlike my river trips, this climb doesn't involve much assessment of the place or myself. I'm barely aware of what's going on. It's all about trust. Good friends have tied the knots, climbed the lead, and put in the protection. I'm just making sure every carabiner near me is locked tight. Belayed by the lead climber above me, I know that if I peel off the rock, I'll fall about six inches and just start climbing again. Still, I hate heights and have to control my breathing. I look down and imagine how if everything went south, I would make my last splash in Sespe Creek, just a few miles upstream from the start of the wilderness kayaking run. After obsessing about boating the Sespe, I'd die in a six-inch-deep mid-August puddle.

Not much chance of that, though. The lead climber took the real risks, looking for the next bolt where a fall would be twice the length of rope strung out between the climber and the last bolt. The route finding for me amounts to looking for the next hand- or toehold, and even that's difficult. As I try to muster the courage to smear a sketchy foot placement, I hear a call from the third person below, "Trust your rubber!" I start laughing, but borrowed, worn-out climbing shoes don't inspire trust, and my leg starts to dance on its own out of nervousness and fatigue—Elvis leg. I take a breath and make a dyno-move to the next handhold, a sandstone flake. Once stable, I slap the rock and hear hollowness below the flake. I don't pull on it again for fear of peeling it off to rain down on the guy below me. Sandstone isn't the best climbing rock, but Sespe Gorge is a beautiful place. The climbs are fun, even elegant, and the more experienced climbers flow up the face, linking moves seamlessly, finding their way through vision, feel, and intuition trained by experience.

I keep thinking about and giving thanks for the bolts. They weren't here when Chouinard was doing his first ascents. Instead, he was placing protection in sandstone and trusting his ability to make the next move. Even though my climbing ability is far behind my paddling, I can begin to see the connections. Somehow the reward seems tied to the risk, but I'm not sure the risk can be understood solely in physical terms. Who knows where each person's heart reaches the edge or when each begins to feel something new or become fully alive? Still, once I rappel back to the base of the slab and stand safe where I had earlier envisioned a grisly death, I wonder what I'm missing by having so much fun without much risk. Are my perceptions dulled? Is my hold on this place less solid, less confident?

Like Chouinard, Chris Nybo, who may be the Sespe's most frequent kayaker of recent years, moves and speaks with the low-key confidence shared by those who regularly push the boundaries of their own limitations. But while Chouinard gives off a subtle "been there done that" vibe, Nybo's enthusiasm for wilderness experience bubbles forth as if eloquent descriptions could transport his listener.

I first met Nybo as he and two others were loading kayaks onto a truck in Fillmore, near the mouth of the Sespe. I was returning from a solo spring backpacking trip, just as he and his friends had finished their wilderness run. One friend had driven twelve hours from Salt Lake City to boat the Sespe. Their boats were smeared with tar from seeps near Tar Creek, and they seemed in a hurry to strap them down and get moving. The group had hoped to do the trip in two days, but the creek slowed them down and they had run out of food. Now it was past noon on Monday, and having eaten a handful of trail mix for breakfast they were eager for lunch. "I hope my wife remembered to call in sick for me," said Nybo.

Nybo took the time, however, to ask me where I had been hiking, and it became clear that he had been everywhere I had been and many more places as well. He knew the Sespe backcountry by both kayak and foot. He has a thin, wiry build and told of running trails high up near the Topatopa bluffs. Routes that for me are challenging three-day backpacking trips become seven-and-a-half-hour trail runs for him. Like Chouinard, the Sespe for Nybo is more than the creek; it represents wholesomeness and integrity. It's more than the sum of its parts. With enthusiasm equal to his tales of kayaking, he tells of snorkeling in deep pools to watch steelhead and of telemark skiing on snow that will melt to form the Sespe.

When Nybo moved to Southern California from Minnesota, he was a little apprehensive about the usual things—people, traffic, smog—until he discovered the backyard wilderness of the Sespe. "It's the most meaningful place in the world to me," he says. This doesn't surprise me, since many people feel this way who come to know the Sespe well. But when Nybo calls it one of the most remote, rugged, and elusive places in California, I begin running through a mental list of other remote places for comparison. After all, the "inner sanctum" about which he waxes most eloquent is only a few miles above Fillmore and fifty or so crow-fly miles from downtown LA. Remote? To explain, Nybo makes an even more outlandish statement: "The lower portion of the creek is more remote than the headwaters of the Kern." Wait a minute. The Kern River flows south from the highest peaks in the Sierra Nevada through some of the most isolated wilderness in California. The few who kayak this portion of the Kern, and this includes Nybo, must carry their boats and gear about twenty-two miles over the 12,000-foot pass called Whitney Portal. Three days of class v kayaking lead to the Johnsondale Bridge north of the town of Kernville. Nybo waits for this to sink in before he explains. "Last year a guy got hurt on the headwaters run," he says, "and they had him out by helicopter in about four hours. That's not going to happen on the Sespe. Phones don't work down there. There are no trails, and a chopper probably couldn't land in the canyon."

Talking with Nybo is like scouting the Sespe. It seems to accentuate the tension I feel between my attraction to the beauty of the river and my fear of knowing it just a little too intimately. I've already decided not to paddle it, and it doesn't help that Nybo seems to end every other sentence by saying, "You've gotta do it. Maybe not this year, but you've gotta do it." Yet he adds other details that remind me why I've backed off: Two days of class IV and v moves with class VI consequences—namely death and dismemberment—and a forty-foot seal launch (sliding from rock into the river) to avoid the worst portage. Landing at the wrong angle from half that height could easily compress vertebrae. He talks about the mental fatigue of making quick decisions and paddling precisely for three days straight.

I ask Nybo how his wife deals with the risk he takes running the Sespe. He says she prays every night and respects his judgment. Ultimately though, he doesn't think so much about risk as about the wildness of the place itself. Kayaking for Nybo has little to do with the extreme sport used to sell SUVs and soda. For him, the risk is just one aspect of the energy and life flowing from the creek and from the whole of the landscape. I think he's referring to his love for wild places more than to risk-taking when he says, "It's in my blood and it's the essence of who I am. That's not to say you won't read my name in the papers someday, but it's part of who I am." Maybe the Sespe itself is part of who he is.

It's a warm fall day, and I'm sitting beside a clear pool ringed by massive red sandstone boulders in the "inner sanctum." Endangered arroyo toads warm themselves on silt-covered stones, and rainbow trout (maybe steelhead?) fingerlings surface for stranded insects. Upstream, the Sespe trickles down the rockslide into the pool, but it's mostly quiet. The creek's springtime energy has flowed downstream to the ocean. A few streamside sycamores have begun to yellow. I'm cultivating an autumnal melancholy.

Sespe Creek seems so much more benign than in its busy spring runoff. Maybe if I could time the flow perfectly, I find myself thinking. Maybe then the risk-reward ratio would approach something I could live with. But as I look at the boulders whose exposed undercuts and sieves are more visible now than they were in the spring, the whole dilemma replays itself in seconds. I shake old thoughts from my head and slap the rock beside me. No more thinking, for now. Appreciate the moment.

Leaving my warm rock, I adjust my swim goggles and slip beneath the surface of the pool. My ears fill as I enter another world for the length of a held breath. The fingerlings that had darted from my silhouette appearing against the sky now relax a little and swim nearby. Immersion changes things.

I swim slowly into a dark tunnel between boulders. Eight feet above my head, in a tangle of driftwood and debris, shards of yellow plastic wink at me. For a split second I see a kayak. Bleached driftwood logs appear as limbs and bones. Part of me wants to swim back out of the tunnel, but I look closer and finally decide I'm seeing a toy inflatable raft that probably slipped from the grasp of a kid where the road meets the Sespe thirty miles upstream. I imagine the tunnel at high water as a sucking whirlpool, pulling floating objects toward the crux where they wait tangled for the next high water.

I smile at my obsession. I even scout the absence of water; I can't break the habit. Drifting into the sun on the other side of the tunnel, I float on my back and watch a pair of ravens swirl alongside the butte high above me. Listening to the thick liquid sounds beneath the surface, I feel comforted to be in this gentle version of Sespe Creek, weightless for a while, drifting slowly into some new sense of this place. I wonder whether I would appreciate the calm of this moment had I experienced the swift energy of the same creek in spring. Maybe, maybe not. But would even two experiences of this stream be enough?

CHAPTER 9

Bringing It All Back Home

Frogs, Poison, and Stories

*We were the tricksters who mocked the best creations and healed
the wounded in a chemical civilization.*

—GERALD VIZENOR, *Dead Voices*

In my dream I'm beside a small creek with someone I don't recognize, someone about whom I can say, "It was his idea." The creek swims with frogs. Hungry, we decide to eat some frogs but don't know quite how to go about it. My companion suggests a headfirst approach and dares me to try. So, to humor him, I tilt my head back and hold a frog, a live frog, above my open mouth with no intention of swallowing. But frogs are slippery, and they wiggle. So down it slides, kind of like an oyster. No chewing. In my dream I grin. That wasn't so bad. Gimme another frog. Slurp. Then I feel a strange, unsettled feeling. I pull up my shirt and watch little protrusions move across my belly like something from an alien movie. When I open my mouth I hear a faint "*ribbit, ribbit.*" The brush nearby parts and my lovely wife emerges. Like a proud schoolboy bringing home roadkill, I show her my new frog-self. She says quietly, "Oh no," and turns to vomit among the rocks. I stare, utterly failing to comprehend her horror.

I wake up and, to *my* horror, burp.

I hadn't tried to dream of frogs. But how they got into my head, among other things, was no mystery. That evening I had spread out my sleeping bag thirty yards or so from a creek filled with spring run-off and mating, red-legged frogs. As night fell, the frogs began to leave the creek to hunt for mice, tree frogs, and insects. I lay there, reading and sipping my little airplane bottle of tequila, enjoying the stars and the amphibian surround-sound in my far-from-home theater. The grass rattled. They came closer. I would swing the beam of my headlamp around, but I never spotted them. The thought of rolling over onto a species listed by the feds as threatened flashed through my sleepy mind. Those sneaky, precious frogs caused just enough anxiety to agitate my subconscious into mixing ribbitting reality with dreamscapes.

Earlier that day, I had hiked by myself into the Sespe backcountry. I had spent hours brush-battling, missing switchbacks, and smearing deer ticks from the back of my neck. Recent snow, ice, and high winds had snapped whole hillsides of chamise and scrub oak branches, and the damage seemed especially bad along the trail where the brush had no support on one side. After all the hard work, I didn't get to where I thought I was going, and finally I stood still at dusk to read the story written in a meadow by a seasonal stream.

Ribbons of frog spawn drifted in the gentle current. As my eyes adjusted to the colors of water, weeds, mud, and reflections, I found a couple of breeding pairs, the males smaller than the females but locked on, embracing them from behind just below their arms. A few other frogs peeked from holes near the stream. From my haunches I watched them for a while, but they were not like TV nature programs. They didn't move or do anything entertaining. Unable to restrain myself, I poked one gently. No reaction. Chastising myself, I stood up and noticed all at once that the stream was in terrible condition. Its banks were mashed to mud by hooves. Cow pies littered the banks and befouled the water. I glanced back at the first breeding pair and saw that they were nestled in pool made by a hoofprint. Just upstream, the current picked away at a splotch of cow shit. I walked a little ways and laid out my sleeping bag.

I wondered: if a female California red-legged frog (*Rana aurora draytonii*) lays two thousand to five thousand eggs in a single mass, would cattle returning to this stream tomorrow lower the 1 percent chance a hatched egg has of reaching adulthood under good conditions? A statistical koan.

I was looking at an old, well-known story in the West. Grazing on public lands is institutionalized, and this was certainly not the first time I'd seen and experienced the impact. Twice while kayaking I've seen dead cows floating in national forest rivers. Once my friend Mike and I were run off trail by a rumbling herd of longhorns in the Golden Trout Wilderness in the southern Sierra Nevada. I've seen many other trampled streams. But I was still surprised to see this one, here in the middle of the Sespe Condor Sanctuary. I couldn't believe grazing would be allowed here.

And it turns out it isn't. A phone call the next week revealed that the cattle are probably left over from a grazing allotment in the 1950s. They're as wild and rangy as deer but considerably more destructive and sloppy. The ranger told me that about five years ago there were occasional reports of a wild bull threatening hikers. My notetaking paused as I thought back to sleeping tentless on the open ground.

But even with the wild cattle, the frogs up in the Sespe have it good compared to some of their cousins closer to the cities. Bullfrogs—non-native predators of the red-leggeds—don't seem to have made it up to the high country yet. Moreover, this land is highly protected. It won't be bulldozed for look-alike Mediterranean-style, tile-roofed houses. Up here in the mountains, the frogs live out their lives dodging the occasional hoof. A few miles south, along the Santa Clara River, the frogs are fewer and live tougher lives, but they are making a big splash.

Along the Santa Clara, the frogs play a role in the effort to stop, or at least limit, the Newhall Ranch development, which proposes to build twenty-two thousand homes. Both developers and opponents of the project watched with great interest when in 1999 a coalition of environmental groups sued the U.S. Fish and Wildlife Service for failing to designate critical habitat for the red-legged frog as required by the Endangered Species Act. In response to the lawsuit, the agency proposed designation of 5.4 million acres throughout the state in the fall of 2000.

The designation, of course, drew a great deal of criticism, since some of the land, including that along the Santa Clara, was privately owned. Under the Endangered Species Act, if private landowners plan activities on their land that require federal permits or receive federal funds, they must consult with regulatory agencies concerning the effects of the activities on the frogs. Developers claimed the economic impact would be devastating not only to builders but also to the state economy. Later, economists hired by Fish and Wildlife estimated the economic impact to be relatively insignificant—$9–13 million spread over ten years statewide. The Building Industry Association of Southern California argued that the economists grossly underestimated the true costs. In response, the Center for Biodiversity, one of the groups that had sued Fish and Wildlife to prompt the designation, suggested that the analysis had actually underestimated the economic benefits of healthy ecosystems and natural flood control. The debate goes on, conducted mostly by lawyers on both sides.

Meanwhile, rough places above the Santa Clara River are being graded plain, and life for the lowland cousins of the Sespe frogs inches closer to the edge. The Newhall Ranch development proposes to become over the next third of a century a complete "community," with schools, supermarkets, Starbucks, and all the rest. The new city will be neat and clean. No doubt there will be rules prohibiting residents from parking cars on the streets or painting exteriors garish colors. There will be a list of plants approved for landscaping. It will be proclaimed a safe place to raise kids, the only dangers being boredom or that by dinnertime they might forget which look-alike house they should go home to.

Though Sespe frogs in the mountains to the north may be safe from bulldozers, their lives are far from simple. Like amphibians everywhere, they are vulnerable to the ultraviolet radiation that slips through the thinning ozone layer. I don't mean to be blithe when I remind myself that they can't wear sun hats and sunscreen. Our technological bandages don't work for them. Furthermore, since frogs breathe through their skins and are thus exceptionally vulnerable to environmental pollutants, it is also possible that exposure to pesticides disrupts their nervous and reproductive systems. How are they exposed to pesticides deep in a wilderness area? Wind, maybe. When I feel a stiff afternoon breeze blast up the canyons from the Santa Clara Valley, I wonder what it could carry with it from the agricultural fields below. Near the mouth of Sespe Creek and the town of Fillmore, there are parcels of land that, according to 1999 statistics, receive pesticide doses as high as 35,000 pounds per year (Californians for Pesticide Reform). When I suggest that frogs in the upper Sespe may be affected by these chemicals, I'm speculating, but not wildly. A recent study in the Sierra Nevada suggests that organophosphate pesticides such as diazonin and chlorpyrifos waft with the prevailing winds into the mountains from the San Joaquin Valley (Zabik and Seiber). The toxins damage amphibian nervous systems and cause frogs to die of respiratory failure. In Yosemite National Park, more than half the frogs tested had the two pesticides in their bodies (Milius). Frog researcher Carlos Davidson's spatial analysis of red-legged frog habitat and prevailing wind patterns strongly suggests that wind-borne agricultural chemicals have contributed to population declines.

The story of the frogs in the high Sespe meadow teaches me what John Muir understood long ago: tug on one thing and you find it hitched to everything in the universe.

Pollution was not on my mind when I hiked up into the Sespe, except insofar as I was trying to escape it temporarily. Subconsciously, I wanted to cross an imaginary border into the wild and forget smog and schoolwork for a while. I wasn't looking for connections so much as a separation. But I made a small concession—I brought a book, thinking I would get a little work done. When I opened the book that night to the growing chorus of frogs, I did not expect each to lend insight to the other.

Wrapped in my sleeping bag on a rock, I reread *Dead Voices,* a novel by the trickster author Gerald Vizenor. I would be discussing the book with a class the following week, and I was stumped. I wanted to avoid teaching the novel in a way that would contradict everything it had to offer. I was afraid of becoming a dead voice. I wanted to avoid shining too much light on the novel's play of ambiguous shadows. Like tricksters in mythic stories, Vizenor's are wild, comic, and irrepressible. They cavort on the borders and at the treelines to help us hear, and maybe retell, the stories of the world we've come to accept. Like Naanabozho, the Anishinaabe trickster in stories from Vizenor's northern Minnesota birthplace, Vizenor's characters take a bit of mud or dung and cast it about the floodwaters to create new islands on which everyone can live. They are comic liberators. But the stories themselves are tricksters, too. Like frogs, they are not easy to grasp. They slip away just when you think you have a handle on them. In the classroom, I wanted to cultivate the book's sense of creativity and endless possibility.

The narrator of *Dead Voices,* a professor of tribal philosophies, meets Bagese, an old woman who lives in an apartment next to a bus stop in Oakland, California. She reeks of sweat and urine. She's the kind of old lady people cross sidewalks to avoid, holding their breath as they pass. But she's not lonely, exactly, for she has the stories that connect her to the natural world, even in the city. The narrator describes her as "a natural contradiction in a cold and chemical civilization" (7). Bagese drums on the professor's head and appears as a bear in mirrors. She has stories to tell. "The secret," the professor reports, "was not to pretend, but to see and hear the real stories behind the words, the voices of the animals in me, not the definitions of the words alone" (7).

In each chapter, Bagese shows the narrator how to enter the imaginative worlds of animals who struggle to survive in a chemical civilization. Gradually, the narrator begins to understand and to cross boundaries he had accepted as real—between the city and the wild, between humans and animals. Vizenor tugs the reader's ears with humor. His metaphors encourage readers to think like tricksters who bring wild words from the treelines to the cities. They help us find our way out of the cage we walked into when we assented to scientific injunctions against anthropomorphism.

A week after the frog dream, and the morning I was to teach *Dead Voices,* I had arrived on campus to find a man in a space suit spraying chemicals on the ground around the prefab building that holds my office. With the sun bright and the birds singing, he looked comical, like someone showing up at the wrong time for a Halloween party. But men in space suits make me nervous, especially when I'm not wearing one myself. I tried to accept the surrealistic quality of the morning as a small compensation for being part of a way of life that accepts chemical invasions as normal and inevitable.

The spraying was, of course, business as usual, a follow-up to the termite tenting the week before. Though most of the building's human residents were quite willing to let the termites have the building, which was officially "temporary" in any case, we had acted as directed. We took away our plants and left file and desk drawers open to let the poison gas in and hopefully out. Faced with an imminent chemical solution to the problem of termites, others and I worried and asked urgent questions that mostly had to do with our own well-being. We listened to the assurances of the exterminators and the rational explanations of administrators: it's harmless, it's part of the lease agreement, it's the most economically feasible alternative. We didn't imagine how the little battle looked from other points of view—for instance, that of the opossums who were gassed along with the termites. A week later, they were slowly decaying in a hidden place beneath the floor. It seemed like tragicomic justice to work daily with the fragrant reminder of our own violence and lack of imagination. We laughed at the irony of the situation, but it would have been better for the 'possums if humor had shaped our future rather than focused our hindsight.

Still, as I sat in my office preparing for class, the man in the space suit helped me awaken to connections between Vizenor and the frog dream, between the city and the Sespe. It occurred to me that I should take the next step, with Vizenor's words for inspiration: "We were the connection to creation, the last season in the treelines, and we landed our best stories in the cities." In the city, at my desk, I shut my eyes and tried to begin a story by imagining frog voices. I heard the elder frog, El Rojo, who despite the pesticide seeping through his skin still breathes out memories of frog culture and history. He says he feels stories on the wind of cannibal bullfrogs from afar, and he excites the youngsters with tales of narrow escapes. "They are to us what we are to tree frogs," he acknowledges. He smiles at his mate La Colorada and tells of love in hoofprints, rationalizing what cannot be avoided: "Cow hooves are our lightning," he proclaims. "They never strike the same place twice."

Hearing the ping of a new e-mail message, I opened my eyes. Thinking up stories like Vizenor's revealed the shape of the walls I sometimes build between my reading, teaching, and everyday life. I gesture toward the relevance of literature and the power of words to shape reality even as I fall silent when faced with shapeable events. I glanced at my watch and sighed—but not deeply, due to the 'possums.

And so, after weeks of rain, the day was bright, warm, and breezy as I walked to class. As usual I turned to glance at the hills to look for ravens or red-tails. I saw clown crows in the olive trees nearby and felt a tingle along my spine. I stepped off the sidewalk and cut diagonally across the lawn under the jacaranda tree. Even non-native landscaping offers sanctuary for the foot and spring for the soul. The soft footfalls helped fill me with energy and optimism. I thought, why not take the class and break out of the building to wander the campus taking turns imagining the stories of whatever we see or hear? What better way to respond to *Dead Voices* than to give life to our own? Here along the border between the Verdugo Hills and urban Los Angeles, we could listen carefully and tell of the ambivalence and contradictions that mark our days and ways. We could hone our attention and begin to transform our thinking and our relationships to this small place. We could test the power of words and the depth of our faith. Stories could bring a little of the Sespe to Burbank.

By the time I walked into class, I had time to doubt. I considered what my colleagues might think of my wandering, storytelling class: Ah, there he is, off the deep end during that sabbatical. Too much time in the bush and his brain turned to mush. So this is what passes for education now. I considered my own discomfort and that which my students would no doubt feel. It's not a creative writing class, after all. We were supposed to study literature, not make it. Vizenor writes, "Wordies have forgotten how to hear and when to surrender to nature and their stories" (132).

I paused near the door, reluctant to enter a building whose windows didn't open, one hermetically sealed to block temperature variations and the noise of jets and crows. Every class period we drew the shades to shut out the afternoon sun. Everything seemed to lean toward sterility and safety instead of improvisation and chance. As I put my hand on the door handle, I heard the high, buzzy trill that signals spring. Between the tops of two trees an Allen's hummingbird did his butt-waggle-dive mating dance. Having crossed all manner of borders during a migration from far south, this little bird arrived with the orange blossoms—as it always does—to gather strength for what really counts. I thought of the hummingbird, the frogs, and the Sespe. I opened the door and walked in.

Confluence

Behold the bush burned with fire, and the bush was not consumed.

—Exodus 3:2

On June 1, 2002, the Sespe made the evening news for something other than condors. This time it was fire, and the conditions were perfect: low humidity, moderate winds, rugged terrain, and continuous stands of seventy-year-old climax chaparral. Over the next couple of days, TV reporters noted the Sespe in brief updates between helicopter shots of other, more telegenic blazes that burned homes, forced evacuations, and more clearly fit the fire narratives we've come to expect in California and the rest of the West. While I watched suburban interviews with heroic firefighters battling a primal, malevolent force of nature, the Sespe burned in the background. And I wasn't sure what to feel.

I rehearsed the ecological benefits of fire in my mind. I reminded myself that fire is an integral and necessary part of Southern California landscapes, but I couldn't shake the feeling in my gut that I was losing something. The familiar was going up in smoke; it looked like death, and I felt grief in spite of everything I knew to be true. I was surprised by how much I had internalized popular images of fire replayed in continual news updates from fire fronts around the West. The deaths of firefighters, crashing air tankers, evacuated towns, torched homes, grieving people. These tend to overshadow the comparatively abstract knowledge of fire's inevitability and of the new life that can arise even from violent transformations.

By the time the fire in the Sespe started, I had been looking at the river and its wilderness from many angles for a long time, and things were starting to come together. Instead of seeing one thing at a time, I was learning to trust my peripheral vision to reveal the shapes and shadows of how things fit together. Streams of consciousness I had been following were flowing toward a confluence, but the fire raised some doubts. Maybe the massive fuel buildup would explode into something bigger than the ecosystem had evolved to survive. Maybe the burn would become the catastrophic event that would wipe out the bighorn sheep. Maybe after the fire, the sediment washed down by winter rains would suffocate the steelhead's gravel spawning beds in Sespe Creek. The fire sparked an anxious imagination.

On the evening of June 3, the Wolf Fire had begun to burn up the slope toward Pine Mountain Ridge and east toward the heart of the wilderness. Ground crews were working to cut fire lines by hand and with bulldozers where the terrain would permit. Air tankers and helicopters dropped fire retardant and water. Three days later, on a breezy mid-90-degree day, the fire went on a run and added eight thousand acres to the over ten thousand it had already burned. Fighting the fire became more risky as the fire jumped out ahead of the crews. The incident commander received permission to construct bulldozer lines within the wilderness boundary where machines are usually not permitted.

The fire had burned for a little over a week before higher humidity and lower temperatures helped firefighters gain control. By the time it had been totally contained on June 14, the fire had burned 21,645 acres—a minuscule number compared with other fires this same summer in Colorado, Arizona, Oregon, and the southern Sierra Nevada. Still, between 1,200 and 1,400 personnel were assigned to the fire, and in addition to brush it consumed a total of $15.3 million in fire-fighting costs. Though much of the fire burned in designated wilderness where natural processes are said to reign, I'm sure the fire managers would have put out the first spark if they could have. But they couldn't. For two weeks the fire danced between utter wildness and human management—like the condors, bighorns, bears, frogs, toads, steelhead, and most things in contemporary wilderness areas.

Before the fire was out, the restoration had started. Teams of experts examined the area from the ground and from the air to assess fire severity, hydrologic scenarios, slope stability, damage to roads and trails, endangered plant and animal habitat, and soil hydrophobicity—that is, the tendency of newly burned soil to repel water and increase runoff in winter rains. Ground crews began to undo the work of bulldozers by covering the firebreaks with topsoil containing native seedbeds and pulling brush over the bare earth. To prevent erosion and gullying, crews constructed water bars and berms to direct future runoff away from the dozer lines and trails. Plans were made, pending funding, to wait for fall rains before spreading thirty pounds of coastal lotus seeds collected from above Fillmore. The use of seed from nearby will maintain local plant genetics and reduce the invasion of exotic species.

The fire, however, affected more than the ecology along the upper Sespe; it may have exposed archaeological sites that had been previously inaccessible. With the exposure came the risk of looting. It is well known in California that relic hunters follow fires, despite the potential penalties of $250,000 fines and two years in prison for removing Native American artifacts or disturbing sensitive sites. These are not the type of people who ignorantly take home an arrowhead or potsherd. They are connected to lucrative black markets in which artifacts bring thousands of dollars. To combat the illegal collecting, U.S. Forest Service archaeologists have been conducting their own surveys and have increased monitoring of sensitive sites, perhaps even with motion detectors.

As always, what we see in the Sespe—what we want to do in it and with it—tells us much about the place itself and about ourselves. The river and its wilderness seem at once vulnerable to petty greed and yet powerful beyond human comprehension. What will we do with it? What will we do with ourselves?

Like so many times before, it's early morning and I'm headed from Los Angeles toward the Sespe. Finally, two months after the burn, I'm going to see for myself the effects of the fire. I ease off the gas a few miles from Fillmore so I can take a quick glance up toward the golden fields of Hopper Mountain. Yes, the mountain is still there. Somewhere in its crags and canyons a wild-hatched condor chick—the first of a new generation—stretches its wings, contemplating flight. In a blind near the nest, a biologist is squinting through a spotting scope, nervous but hopeful.

On the other side of town, I pass the Sespe's mouth on my way toward its source. As the highway passes over the last stretch of Sespe Creek just before it joins the Santa Clara River, I don't slow down. I barely glance. The creek bed looks like a gravel pit. Bone-dry boulders and sand lie piled according to the whim of the last storm flow. My mind's eye looks a few miles upstream, away from roads, where a few pools wait for the winter rains. Black bears are starting to follow the creek bed down toward the avocado orchards to put on pounds for the winter. Figures painted on stone persist for another season. I feel like I know a secret when I think of the life of this stream. Seeing Sespe Creek, even dry, reminds me of the cycles it centers. They will continue, I tell myself. Already I know that the fire was part of the happenstance that punctuates an order beyond our human perspectives.

I drive highway 33 north of Ojai and into Rose Valley, and then I start to walk. I take in the wide-angle view of the scene. The gray-green chaparral is especially dry this year, and it contrasts sharply with the bright cottonwood trees and willows along the creek bed. On the other side of the creek the chaparral resumes and follows a rise to the burn line. Beyond, whole mountainsides sit in ashen silence. The sandstone outcrops called Piedra Blanca—fossilized sand dunes 65 million years old—stand bright white like monuments in the charred soil. From a distance, it really does look like a moonscape. I find it hard not to feel the devastation of absence. Where once was so much, there now appears to be nothing. I move closer.

A few minutes down the dusty trail I cross Sespe Creek and approach the fire line on a path carved through seventy-year-old chamise and scrub oak. On either side of me the shrubs form a wall four to six feet overhead. When I peer into the brush, I can't see more than an arm length or two, and light doesn't reach the ground. A rabbit flushes ahead of me on the trail and darts into the underbrush where nothing but a skinny, highly motivated coyote could follow. I walk on, feeling the familiar claustrophobia of so many local trails, and when I reach the fire line the effect is dramatic. Within five yards I move from untouched climax chaparral to scorched earth.

Almost imperceptibly, my spirits begin to lift. I feel a certain release and freedom that I don't quite understand. I walk out into the burn to find something in the real world to hang my emotions on. I stand in the sun breathing slowly. Everything smells like a day-old campfire. I shut my eyes and listen to the ruckus of scrub jays and underneath them the watery chirruping of a flock of quail playing the borders between the fire clearing and good cover. A chattering flock of bushtits flows by in waves, and a flicker sounds the alarm in rhythm with its roller-coaster stroke and glide. I know these things even though I don't see them. This place is far from dead. It's lively, active, on the move.

I can imagine closing my eyes and breathing until the borders between my skin and the outside world dissolve, but it's getting hot, so I move on. Powdery dust and ash swirl at each footfall as I follow the trail through the burn. The chamise and scrub oak that had been ten feet tall have been consumed in some places down to two-inch nubs. In other places the fire has left waist-high charred stems. All together, the stumps seem too few to correspond to the thickness of the pre-burn brush. And amazingly, sprouts of new growth emerge from the blackened roots. This, only two months after the burn in the middle of a dry, rainless summer. Newly green, even the greasewood feels tender.

As I head toward a line of green—a tributary of the Sespe flowing through the middle of the burn—I make side trips to generations of litter that has been exposed. There are glass bottles half melted, anchovy tins with lids peeled back, and beer cans—new ones with push tabs, older ones with pull tabs, and the oldest, a steel can with two triangle punctures, part of its label preserved face down in the dust.

Along the creek, bunchgrass shoots rise from ashy clumps that disintegrate with the slightest touch. Insects cloud above pools filled with charcoal. Deer tracks line the banks. Upstream, the creek runs quick and clear. Fingerling trout dart away from my shadow.

Further along, the sandstone monuments have acted as firebreaks to protect scattered manzanita and oaks. At one point in the trail, amid many boot tracks, I find the prints of a small bear, about the same size as a lion's paw prints three feet away. Tracks everywhere—coyotes, rabbits, rodents, lizards, snakes. Everyone seems to be curious about this newly uncovered territory. Everyone seems to be part of what it will become. I find myself looking for bighorn sheep tracks even though I know I'm probably miles from the nearest sheep. The fire I worried would wipe out my beloved bighorns opened up what looks like fine habitat on the higher ridges. Ironically, the fire was contained just before it could connect with their present habitat, and the sheep may not want to venture through the remaining few miles of thick chaparral to find the new range. But perhaps the drought will make them willing to take higher risks to find good forage. Maybe the scent of new green on the wind will set them out toward the new territory.

Thinking of the bighorns reminds me that I'm learning to think of the Sespe less as my "escape habitat" than as a place that teaches me to be fully alive. Its harshness and beauty burn away the parts of me that threaten to become too old, rigid, and shady. Without the burning, my soul would have no hope of green. I would not want to live without this process happening around and inside me; and yet, the more it occurs the less I seem to need. Sometimes now I think the scent of sage in my front yard does for me what a three-day backpack used to. But even so, I'll keep coming back—in winter rain and snow to watch the creek awaken, in spring to see the postfire riot of wildflowers. After all, we don't have many places like this that have survived beyond reason and probability to tell their own ongoing stories at their own pace. How we listen to the Sespe tell its story is part of how we tell our own.

Acknowledgments

As I've written this book, many people have helped me grasp a little of what they know. Some of them understand the Sespe over such time and in such depth as to remind me that I'm only beginning to understand what it means to know a place. I'm grateful for their generosity, their time spent on the phone, their returned e-mails, and for letting me tag along. Some have gone so far as to read and comment on draft chapters. The book became clearer and more accurate for their attention, and any mistakes still present are mine. Thanks first to Brenda Monsma, whose initial readings and persistent questions spared later readers confusion and effort. Thanks to Rebecca Barbosa, Mike Barth, Roger Bloom, Douglas Burton-Christie, Rick Bury, Yvon Chouinard, Kevin Cooper, Alasdair Coyne, Bronwyn Davie, Jim Davis, Jim Day, Janine McFarland, Michael Moore, John Nichols, Chris Nybo, Bruce Palmer, Tim Palmer, Steve Torres, Mike Vaughan, Morgan Wehtje, and Paul Willis.

I'm also thankful to those at the University of Nevada Press who have helped to bring this book into being, especially Joanne O'Hare for her initial interest and shepherding of the project. I'm grateful to John Mulvihill for sensitive and alert copyediting.

My colleagues at Woodbury University offered support in many ways. Thanks to Doug Cremer, Mary Collins, Phil Pack, Elisabeth Sandberg, and Joye Swan. Woodbury also offered sabbatical support and a summer research grant.

A special level of gratitude goes to my trail companions over the years, especially Mike Chen, Juergen Stockburger, and Brenda: for inspiration and motivation through hot climbs, cold windy nights, ticks, pointless bushwhacking, poison oak, too-deep stream crossings, malfunctioning "whisper-fight" stoves, busted backpacks, tar-stained clothes, and pruned skin from excessive hot spring soaking—the price of admission.

I reserve my deepest gratitude for Brenda, my partner and soul mate. Without her support in so many ways, this would have come to nothing.

Versions of the chapters "Seeing Through Stone" and "Bear in Mind" were published in *ISLE: Interdisciplinary Studies in Literature and Environment* and *Common Ground.* Thanks to their editors, Scott Slovic and Jeff Yule.

References

Abram, David. *The Spell of the Sensuous: Perception and Language in a More-than-Human World.* New York: Vintage, 1996.

American Whitewater. "Safety Code of American Whitewater." http://www.americanwhitewater.org/archive/safety/safety.html (September 2002).

Bean, Lowell John. "Power and Its Applications in Native California." In *California Indian Shamanism,* edited by Bean, 21–32.

———, ed. *California Indian Shamanism.* Menlo Park, Calif.: Ballena Press, 1992.

Bean, Lowell John, and Sylvia Brakke Vane. "The Shamanic Experience." In *California Indian Shamanism,* edited by Bean, 7–19.

Blackburn, Thomas C. *December's Child: A Book of Chumash Oral Narratives Collected by J. P. Harrington.* Berkeley and Los Angeles: University of California Press, 1975.

Blackburn, Thomas C., and Kat Anderson, eds. *Before the Wilderness: Environmental Management by Native Californians.* Menlo Park, Calif.: Ballena Press, 1993.

Bury, Rick. "Too Many Shamans: Ethics and Politics of Rock Art Interpretation." *American Indian Rock Art* 25 (1999): 149–54.

Californians for Pesticide Reform. "Pesticide Use in Ventura County." 1999. http://www.igc.org/cpr/datamaps/maps/ventura.gif (August 2002).

Castillo, Edward D. "Blood Came From Their Mouths: Tongva and Chumash Responses to the Pandemic of 1801." *American Indian Culture and Research Journal* 23, no. 4 (1999): 47–61.

Cleland, Robert G. *The Place Called Sespe.* Privately printed, 1940.

Cone, Marla. "A Wind-Borne Threat to Sierra Frogs." *Los Angeles Times,* 8 December 2000, p. A3.

"A Costly Fire Season." *Forest Magazine* 3, no. 6 (2001): 10–11.

Datta, S., et al. "Pesticides and PCB Contaminants in Fish and Tadpoles from the Kaweah River Basin, California." *Bulletin of Environmental Contamination and Toxicology* 60 (1998): 829–36.

Department of the Interior, Fish and Wildlife Service. "Endangered and Threatened Wildlife and Plants; Proposed Designation of Critical Habitat for the California Red-Legged Frog (*Rana aurora draytonii*); Proposed Rule." *Federal Register,* pt. III, 11 September 2000.

Donne, John. "Meditation XVII." In *Seventeenth-Century Prose and Poetry,* 2d ed., edited by Alexander M. Witherspoon and Frank J. Warnke, 68–69. New York: Harcourt Brace Jovanovich, 1982.

Dosch, Murray W. "Sespe Oil Field." In State of California Division of Oil and Gas, *Summary of Operations, California Oil Fields,* 39–55.

Duncan, David James. "Salmon's Second Coming." *Sierra,* March–April 2000: 31–41.

Eastwood, John S. Chief Engineer. "Report on the Sespe-Piru Power and Water Project of the Sespe Light and Power Company." 6 September 1921. Private collection of John Nichols.

Finney, Kevin, and Jim Edmondson. "Swimming Upstream: Restoring the Rivers and Streams of Coastal Southern California for Southern Steelhead and Other Fishes." Southern California Steelhead Recovery Coalition, 1999. http://www.socalsteelhead.org/frames/steelhead.pdf (May 2002).

Geist, Valerius. *Mountain Sheep: A Study in Behavior and Evolution.* Chicago: University of Chicago Press, 1971.

Grant, Campbell. *The Rock Paintings of the Chumash: A Study of California Indian Culture.* Berkeley and Los Angeles: University of California Press, 1966.

Grumbine, R. Edward. *Ghost Bears: Exploring the Biodiversity Crisis.* Washington, D.C.: Island Press, 1992.

Haslam, Gerald W. *Condor Dreams and Other Fictions.* Reno: University of Nevada Press, 1994.

Hedges, Ken. "Shamanistic Aspects of California Rock Art." In *California Indian Shamanism,* edited by Bean, 67–88.

Heizer, R. F., ed. *Chumash Place Name Lists: Compilations by A. L. Kroeber, C. Hart Merriam, and H. W. Henshaw.* Berkeley: Archaeological Research Facility, Department of Anthropology, 1975.

Hopkins, Gerard Manley. *The Poems of Gerard Manley Hopkins.* 2d ed. Edited by Robert Bridges. New York: Oxford University Press, 1930.

Hudson, Travis, and Thomas C. Blackburn. *The Material Culture of the Chumash Interaction Sphere.* 5 vols. Menlo Park, Calif.: Ballena Press; Santa Barbara, Calif.: Santa Barbara Museum of Natural History, 1982.

Hudson, Travis, Thomas Blackburn, and Rosario Culetti, eds. *The Eye of the Flute: Chumash Traditional History and Ritual as Told by Fernando Librado Kitsepawit to John P. Harrington.* Santa Barbara, Calif.: Santa Barbara Museum of Natural History, 1977.

Hudson, Travis, and Ernest Underhay. *Crystals in the Sky: An Intellectual Odyssey Involving Chumash Astronomy, Cosmology, and Rock Art.* Menlo Park, Calif.: Ballena Press; Santa Barbara, Calif.: Santa Barbara Museum of Natural History, 1978.

Hughes, Timothy. "Chumash Sites Exposed to New Risks." *Los Angeles Times,* 23 June 2002, p. B1.

Hyde, Lewis. *The Gift: Imagination and the Erotic Life of Property.* New York: Vintage, 1979.

Jackson, Robert H., and Edward Castillo. *Indians, Franciscans, and Spanish Colonization: The Impact of the Mission System on California Indians.* Albuquerque: University of New Mexico Press, 1995.

LaPena, Frank. "A Native American's View of Rock Art." In *Ancient Images on Stone: Rock Art of the Californias,* edited by Jo Anne Van Tilburg. Los Angeles: Rock Art Archive, Institute of Archaeology, University of California, 1983.

Lewis, Henry T. "Patterns of Indian Burning in California: Ecology and Ethnohistory." In *Before the Wilderness,* edited by Blackburn and Anderson, 55–116.

Lippard, Lucy. Foreword to *Marks in Place: Contemporary Responses to Rock Art,* edited by Lucy Lippard. Albuquerque: University of New Mexico Press, 1988.

Lopez, Barry. *Of Wolves and Men.* New York: Scribner, 1978.

Los Padres National Forest. "Wolf Fire BAER and Suppression Rehab Teams' Summary of Activities." 13 August 2002. http://www.r5.fed.us/lospadres/news/fire/baer_activity.html.

McCarty, Craig W., and James A. Bailey. *Habitat Requirements of Desert Bighorn Sheep.* Special Report No. 69. Colorado Division of Wildlife, 1994.

McMillan, Ian. *Man and the California Condor: The Embattled History and Uncertain Future of North America's Largest Free-Living Bird.* New York: Dutton, 1968.

Milius, Susan. "Wafting Pesticides Taint Far-Flung Frogs." *Science News* 158, no. 25 (2000): 391.

Mitchell, Wm. Spencer. "An Evaluation of Air and Other Drilling Media in Tar Creek and Topatopa Areas of Sespe Oil Field." In State of California Division of Oil and Gas, *Summary of Operations, California Oil Fields,* 57–64.

Muir, John. *The Mountains of California.* 1894. New York: Penguin, 1985.

Outland, Charles F. *Mines, Murders, and Grizzlies: Tales of California's Ventura Backcountry.* Ventura, Calif.: Ventura Historical Society, 1986.

Palmer, Tim. *The Wild and Scenic Rivers of America.* Washington, D.C.: Island Press, 1993.

Perry, M. P., J. W. Dole, and S. A. Holl. "Analysis of the Diets of Mountain Sheep from the San Gabriel Mountains, California." *California Department of Fish and Game* 73: 156–62.

Phillips, David, and Hugh Nash. *The Condor Question: Captive or Forever Free?* San Francisco: Friends of the Earth, 1981.

Polakovic, Gary. "Deaths of the Little Bighorns." *Los Angeles Times Online,* 29 August 2001.

Powell, R. A., J. W. Zimmerman, and D. E. Seaman. *Ecology and Behaviour of North American Black Bears: Home Ranges, Habitat, and Social Organization.* London: Chapman and Hall, 1997.

Reisner, Marc. *Cadillac Desert: The American West and Its Disappearing Water.* New York: Penguin, 1987.

Rintoul, William. *Drilling Through Time: 75 Years With California's Division of Oil and Gas.* Sacramento: California Department of Conservation, 1990.

Sespe Light and Power Company. "Articles of Incorporation." 31 March 1915. Private collection of John Nichols.

Shepard, Paul. *Nature and Madness.* Athens: University of Georgia Press, 1982.

———. *The Others: How Animals Made Us Human.* Washington, D.C.: Island Press, 1996.

Shepard, Paul, and Barry Sanders. *The Sacred Paw: The Bear in Nature, Myth, and Literature.* New York: Viking, 1985.

Smith, Dick. *Condor Journal: The History, Mythology, and Reality of the California Condor.* Edited by Olive Kingston Smith. Santa Barbara, Calif.: Capra Press; Santa Barbara, Calif.: Santa Barbara Museum of Natural History, 1978.

Snyder, Noel, and Helen Snyder. *The California Condor: A Saga of Natural History and Conservation.* San Diego: Academic Press, 2000.

State of California Division of Oil and Gas. *Summary of Operations, California Oil Fields: Fifty-Third Annual Report of the State Oil and Gas Supervisor.* Vol. 53, no. 1. San Francisco: 1967.

Stegner, Wallace. "Wilderness Letter." 1960. In *A Forest of Voices: Conversations in Ecology,* edited by Chris Anderson and Lex Runciman. Mountain View, Calif.: Mayfield, 2000.

Storer, Tracy I., and Lloyd P. Tevis Jr. *California Grizzly.* 1955. Berkeley and Los Angeles: University of California Press, 1996.

Timbrook, Jan, John R. Johnson, and David D. Earle. "Vegetation Burning by the Chumash." In *Before the Wilderness,* edited by Blackburn and Anderson, 117–49.

Valdez, Raul, and Paul R. Krausman. *Mountain Sheep of North America.* Tucson: University of Arizona Press, 1999.

Vizenor, Gerald. *Dead Voices.* Norman: University of Oklahoma Press, 1992.

Wehtje, Morgan (wildlife biologist with California Department of Fish and Game). Interview by author. 13 October 2000

Whitley, David S. *A Guide to Rock Art Sites: Southern California and Southern Nevada.* Missoula, Mont.: Mountain Press, 1996.

Zabik, J. M., and J. N. Seiber. "Atmospheric Transport of Organophosphate Pesticides from California's Central Valley to the Sierra Nevada Mountains." *Journal of Environmental Quality* 22 (1993): 80–90.